Practical Skills and Clinical Management of Alcoholism and Drug Addiction

Practical Skills and Clinical Management of Alcoholism and Drug Addiction

Samuel B. Obembe, M.B;B.S., C.A.D.C.
Cognitive Insight Inc. Alcoholism & Drug Addiction Treatment, Portland, Oregon, U.S.A.

AMSTERDAM • BOSTON • HEIDELBERG • LONDON • NEW YORK • OXFORD
PARIS • SAN DIEGO • SAN FRANCISCO • SINGAPORE • SYDNEY • TOKYO

ELSEVIER

Elsevier
32 Jamestown Road, London NW1 7BY
225 Wyman Street, Waltham, MA 02451, USA

First edition 2012
Copyright © 2012 Elsevier Inc. All rights reserved

Notices
Knowledge and best practice in this field are constantly changing. As new research and experience broaden our understanding, changes in research methods, professional practices, or medical treatment may become necessary.

Practitioners and researchers must always rely on their own experience and knowledge in evaluating and using any information, methods, compounds, or experiments described herein. In using such information or methods they should be mindful of their own safety and the safety of others, including parties for whom they have a professional responsibility.

To the fullest extent of the law, neither the Publisher nor the authors, contributors, or editors, assume any liability for any injury and/or damage to persons or property as a matter of products liability, negligence or otherwise, or from any use or operation of any methods, products, instructions, or ideas contained in the material herein.

British Library Cataloguing-in-Publication Data
A catalogue record for this book is available from the British Library

Library of Congress Cataloging-in-Publication Data
A catalog record for this book is available from the Library of Congress

ISBN: 978-0-12-398518-7

For information on all Elsevier publications
visit our website at store.elsevier.com

This book has been manufactured using Print On Demand technology. Each copy is produced to order and is limited to black ink. The online version of this book will show color figures where appropriate.

Working together to grow
libraries in developing countries

www.elsevier.com | www.bookaid.org | www.sabre.org

ELSEVIER   BOOK AID
International   Sabre Foundation

Contents

Note to Readers

Practical Skills and Clinical Management of Alcoholism and Drug Addiction is a synopsis (summary) of causes and clinical management of alcoholism and drug addiction enhanced with practical skills and other awareness resources. The intent of the clinical literature in this book is primarily to educate, motivate, and dispel myths that enable addiction.

The final diagnosis of drug addiction is in itself just the tip of the iceberg. The primary diseases or circumstances that largely constitute the vulnerability to addiction are indeed the essence worthy of treatment to minimize or eradicate addiction. These provocative factors are genetic (familial) predisposition, mental illness, family dysfunction, unhealthy lifestyles, and other countless negative environmental conditions that cause and propagate alcoholism and drug addiction, a complex disease of genetic and/or acquired etiologies. Thus, it is about treatment, NOT punishment.

This book provides information from researched facts to address this perennial issue. It sheds light on causes of alcoholism and drug addiction that broaden the scope of clinical management of the disease. Also, it punctuates the literature with practical skills that contribute to knowledge in clinical management, and gives insight to patients and their challenges.

It is our ultimate responsibility to ensure a healthy, safe, and peaceful society for us, our children, and generations yet to come.

A *real crisis* that remains is that addiction is seen by too many as a reprehensible moral weakness, instead of being recognized as a disease or a medical condition. Despite recent advances in treatment methods, social stigma and misconceptions about addiction still persist. As more humane laws are enacted to support the medical consensus, public perceptions about addiction will change. Family members, friends, employers, health care professionals, and behavioral therapists must become proactive in educating the public.

At present, many who suffer from real and pervasive consequences of addiction tend to lead secret lives, obsessed with fears that their "weakness" may be revealed. Until such time as we can dispel these stereotypes and dispense with prejudice and discrimination, addicts and their families will suffer needlessly. And we, as a people, will be diminished by their pain and reaction. The stigmatization of these victims must end. We owe it to our families, neighbors, communities, and to ourselves.

Dr. Samuel B. Obembe, M.B;B.S., C.A.D.C
Website: Cognitiveinsightinc.com
Contact: www.info@cognitiveinsightinc.com
www.insightinc20@gmail.com

My Story

A multifaceted dimension of life events serves as the inspiration for writing of this book. The drug addiction of my godson impacted me deeply, revealing my ignorance and judgmental attitude toward him. He has a family history of alcoholism. His grandfather was a recovering alcoholic. His mother and brother are alcohol abusers. He is cross-addicted to prescription and street drugs such as oxycodone, cocaine, and heroin in particular. As of today, the good news is that he has been sober for 2 years, secured a job, and taken responsibility for his 9-year-old daughter.

During his difficult time, I was very hard on him. Could it be an epiphany that drove a feeling of guilt and remorse into me? Something was responsible for my decision to check into an academic institution to study "Addiction and its Management."

I was aware of a fact that over 50% of my colleagues were in sobriety and at risk for relapse. As a physician, my curiosity and preparedness for any eventuality was undoubted. The adventure was worthy of the experience. It challenged, educated, and changed my perspective toward victims of this disease.

My closest colleague in the class was a student from Reed College. He was so brilliant and interesting in every aspect of life. He experienced emotional shifts or alternations through all seasons that were reflected in his demeanor. The severity of depression during winter and elation in summer was of great concern. He confided in me of his struggle with the disease and how the weather extremes exacerbated the illness. For him, the exhibited symptoms are distinctively characteristic of bipolar disorder, a mental and emotional disturbance, and were responsible for his vulnerability to drug addiction. He further shared with me how he would be spending his winter in Hawaii. He overdosed and died 6 months later.

Another close colleague that I related with in the class was quite intelligent with in-depth knowledge and understanding of his clients' situations, in spite of his own struggle with drug addiction. His brilliant presentations at the weekly meetings of counselors were an apparent conviction of his strength in sobriety and recovery. Unfortunately, he overdosed on heroin and died over a stressful breakup with his girlfriend.

The third relapsed and checked into a treatment center. He had a history of multiple relapses in the past 5 years.

These are evidence of the recurring nature of the disease: a "loss of control" due to compulsive brain craving for addictive chemical substance(s) as a result of neurochemical transmitter imbalance that transforms into the dysfunctional mindset of an addict. The magnitude of devastation to the client, his/her family, and friends is most of the time beyond the darkest realm of imagination. There is a critical need for consistent or possibly lifetime treatment coupled with a healthy lifestyle.

My education in this field of health care provides me with an insight into causative factors of drug addiction that ranges from genetics, mental illness, stress, lifestyles, and other aggravating factors. It also affords me a sound knowledge and vast clinical experience in treatment management.

The treatment is about cognitive restructuring. This entails medication therapy, especially in cases of dual diagnosis (i.e., anxiety, depression, schizophrenia, and other mental illnesses primary to drug addiction) as clinically recommended, and psychotherapy (individual and group therapy, aftercare programs, etc.), an essential treatment tool in every case.

The success of this treatment model often promotes self-enhancement and self-empowerment that translate into positive behavior modification. Prognosis is best when a client takes the first step: admission to a problem with alcohol and/or drug, an exercise in personal responsibility, and an enduring commitment to treatment. Relapse could be avoided or minimized by client's unflinching determination and aspiration for treatment, consistent care support, and healthy lifestyle.

Clinical experience from academic and social interaction with vulnerable friends, caring for abusers and addicts, spurs me to put it all in a precise context titled *Practical Skills and Clinical Management of Alcoholism and Drug Addiction*. I hope this clinical literature achieves its ultimate goal of awareness, healthy lifestyle, and a path to treatment of this deadly disease of our time.

A Holistic Approach to Clinical Management

The ultimate goal of this book is a comprehensive clinical management.

The essence of this book is to educate, raising awareness of the devastation of addiction and offering treatment management that is holistic in approach. The treatment technique involves identifying the multiple pathologies that drive alcohol and drug addiction, designing a treatment plan that mitigates the enabling pathological forces and promotes maintenance of a healthy state through a continuum of treatment and support programs.

Causes of alcoholism and drug addiction are vast and complex. Researchers are still making new discoveries and treatment modalities to battle the disease.

The critical tools of holistic clinical management are psychological, involving mental restructuring techniques such as individual and/or group psychotherapy/counseling and support groups. Emphasis is placed on practical skills that are effective teaching tools.

Medical and psychological procedures which entail screening and treatment for related diseases or vulnerability factors such as genetic predisposition, mental illness, post-traumatic stress disorder (PTSD) and other numerous negative environmental elements, have immensely contributed to knowledge of causes and clinical management of alcoholism and drug addiction.

Nutritional depletion and deficiency are often a complication of alcoholism and drug addiction. The resulting nutritional dysfunctional dynamic serves as a significant driver of the pathophysiological processes of addiction. A healthy lifestyle supported by exercise and meeting nutritional needs that are vital to health can reverse the abnormal process, and present a crucial front in the treatment of alcoholism and drug addiction.

Besides the treatment strategy, the book enlightens in all related aspects of alcohol and drug addiction: psychoactive drugs, their effects and properties; sharing of the author's clinical experiences; and practical skills and other educative resources that are beneficial to the management of alcoholism and drug addiction.

Disclaimer

The ideas, clinical approaches, and suggestions put forward in this book are not a substitute for consultation with physicians, psychiatrists, psychotherapists, counselors, and so forth.

Supervision is an absolute necessity in all health matters.

Thanks

To my caring big sister, Mrs. Funke Akin-Williams (nee Obembe)
To my lovely daughter Layo, and to my gentle and "cool" sons, Lade and Lolu
And to my favorite librarians, Viet Tran and Ryan Ellis.
Love you all.

1 Addiction and its Etiology

The word "addiction" is loosely applied in social expression to indicate self-indulgence: cravings for food, drink, behavior, things, or places of interest. Basic human cravings are food, water, sex, and sleep. We frequently make these choices because of pleasures derived, but to a large extent within a normal range of consumption without dependency. But we shiver when faced with the intense, destructive consequences of addiction.

Some of the most devastating addictions involve gambling, alcohol, and psychoactive drugs. Other forms of addiction include eating, shopping, sex, the Internet, work, video games, and so forth. These behaviors may impact a person differently, but they can be just as devastating as alcohol and substance dependence.

The content of this literature directly and explicitly addresses the causes and treatment of alcoholism and drug addiction. Also, it places emphasis on practical skills that are essential in treatment management. The intent is to convey the message in synopsis but with clarity, which raises awareness to the causes and destructive effects of alcohol and drug addiction, contributes to the knowledge in management of the disease, dispels related social stigma through scientific insight into the nature of the disease, and provides proper guidance to achieving long-term, possibly life-time sobriety and recovery.

Compulsive consumption of alcohol and/or psychoactive drugs is defined as chemical dependence. This behavior is a shift from an impulsive (tendency to act on a whim—high vulnerability) to a compulsive behavior (a force-driven irrational impulse). The compulsion involves a loss of control in limiting intake of alcohol or psychoactive drugs of choice. This may involve impaired brain function, neuron damage, or synaptic dysfunction. The disease is found in the mesolimbic dopamine system, also referred to as the "pleasure pathway" or "reward system."

The two primary indicators of alcohol and drug addiction are: (1) tolerance—an increase in the amount of intake to produce the same pleasure or a need for a higher dose to elicit the same effect; and (2) withdrawal symptoms—in the course of acute or chronic abuse of psychoactive drugs or alcohol, a physical or physiological adaptation occurs. A sudden or abrupt cessation of intake will precipitate acute physical or physiological symptoms: body pain, nausea, chills, vomiting, and depression. These can be devastating and are most often coupled with negative emotional state. Human compulsion is a pathological driving force which seeks attainment of "pleasure" feelings. The ultimate goal of this force is addiction and this state is sustained by a fear of withdrawal symptoms. This vicious cycle perpetuates addictive habit.

These are the primary operative elements of addiction. There are specific stages of chemical dependence which culminate into this disease state:

- Impulsive to compulsive behavior (loss of control of use) or neuronal damage.
- Psychobiological pathology: physiological and psychological dependence.
- Withdrawal stage—irritable discomfort from sudden cessation of use ("cold turkey" symptoms).

Practical Skills and Clinical Management of Alcoholism and Drug Addiction.
DOI: http://dx.doi.org/10.1016/B978-0-12-398518-7.00001-8

Formal addiction is an adaptation of the psychoactive substance into the "normal" physiology of the body. This dynamic involves physical compulsion by dramatic changes in brain function as a result of destructive effect due to constant and prolonged exposure to the chemical substance. Addiction is a pathological condition: a medical condition or a disease.

Causes could be intrinsic (genetic or familial) or extrinsic (environmental; unhealthy lifestyle, peer group, etc.) predisposing factors.

Griffith Edwards, DM, and Milton M. Gross, MD, provided a definition of chemical dependence syndrome in 1976. They described the essential elements of the syndrome as "*a repertoire of drinking behavior; salience of drink-seeking behavior; increased tolerance to alcohol; repeated withdrawal symptoms; repeated relief or avoidance of withdrawal symptoms by further drinking; subjective awareness of a compulsion to drink; reinstatement of the syndrome after abstinence. All these elements exist in degree, thus giving the syndrome a range of severity; one clinical element may reflect underlying psychobiological happenings of several types and different clinical elements may be partial descriptions of the same underlying psychobiological process*" (Edwards & Gross, 1976).

This is an explicit definition of chemical dependence syndrome—combined symptoms that characterize the disease. And it is this concept of clinical presentation by these experts that inspired a formal recognition of the syndrome. Multiple authorities agree with the syndrome as a clinical definition of alcohol and drug addiction: International Classification of Disease (ICD-10) and Other Health Problems Manual (World Health Organization, 1992) and Diagnostic and Statistical Manual of Mental Disorders Fourth Edition, Text Revision (DSM-IV TR).

Because addiction is interchangeable with the more specific terminology of chemical dependence, I may apply either term to convey the same meaning.

1.1   Definition and Characteristics of Alcoholism and Drug Addiction (Substance Dependence)

Many definitions have been given to addiction which sometimes lack the specific operative words, while some have done justice to it. Morse and Flavin's (1992) definition of addiction published in the *Journal of the American Medical Association* (vol. 68, No. 8) states that addiction is a primary, progressive, chronic disease with genetic, psychosocial, and environmental factors influencing its development and manifestation. The disease is often progressive and fatal. It is characterized by impaired control overuse of the substance, preoccupation with the substance, use of the substance despite adverse consequences, and distortion to thinking. This definition stands as the guiding principle of treatment centers and substance-abuse counselors.

Addiction could also be conceptualized as a demonstration of a pathological relationship with any mood-altering experience that results in ongoing, recurring life-damaging negative consequences. Pathologies such as denial, delusion entrenched with other defense mechanisms that are so crazy and irrational to the objective mind can occur. Life-damaging negative consequences and health problems due to alcoholism are depicted in Figure 2.1. Drug addiction is just as devastating, possibly more immediate, and often results in fatality. Legal problems are also most often consequences of abuse and addiction to drugs.

Loss of self-respect, respect of family or peers, jobs; irrational cognition, argumentative and negative attitude are social and economic downfalls due to alcoholism and drug addiction.

The American Psychiatric Association (APA) definition of alcohol and drug addiction is based on clinical symptoms. It states that addiction or dependence is present in an individual that demonstrates any three or more of the following symptoms at any time in the same 12-month period:

1. Tolerance: This is defined as a need to substantially increase the amount of intake of the psychoactive substance in order to achieve the same desired effect. This could be inversely expressed as a markedly diminished effect from same amount of substance that on prior intake had a desired effect.
2. Withdrawal: Abrupt cessation of substance intake manifests characteristic signs and symptoms of the withdrawal syndrome. Intake of same or closely related psychoactive substance could produce a relief or avoidance of withdrawal symptoms.
3. Larger amount of substance is taken for a longer period, indicating loss of control over setting limit of use.
4. Persistent desire to use psychoactive substance and inability or failure to quit or cut down on substance use.
5. Preoccupation or obsession with activities to obtain the substance, use of the substance, or failure of plan or intention to quit the use and recovery from the life-threatening symptoms of the psychoactive substance.
6. Consequential reduction or complete withdrawal from social, occupational, or recreational activities predicated on substance use.
7. The substance use is intensified as tolerance escalates in spite of the recurrent physical and psychological problems that are caused by the persistent use.

In view of these definitions and the characterization of addiction, it is essential to identify the differences among users of addictive/psychoactive substances. They could be classified into three groups:

1. Social user
2. Alcohol/substance abuser
3. Addict

Social user: He/She uses alcohol and/or drugs simply to enhance the pleasure of normally pleasurable situations. The social user experiences the following:

- No negative consequences
- No surprises or unpredictability
- No loss of control
- No complaints
- No thoughts of or need for limit setting

Alcohol/Substance abuser: He/She uses to enhance pleasure and/or compensate for something negative, such as physical or emotional pain, insecurity, fear, anger, and so on. The substance abuser experiences:

• Occasional negative consequences that are not repeated
• Limit setting that is adhered to
• Complaints are heard and dealt with

Addict: He/She uses to celebrate, compensate, or for any other reason, legitimate or not. The addict experiences some or all of the following:

• Negative consequences are recycled
• Limit setting and promises to self or others are broken
• Complaints are denied and/or not heard
• Reliable symptoms of addictive diseases become more evident
• Continued use despite negative consequences
• Loss of control, as in more use than planned (broken limits)
• Unpredictability, as in use despite plan not to use (broken promises)
• Compulsivity/preoccupation in thinking
• Denial; use of defenses to maintain denial
• Build up of (or 'break' in) tolerance
• Remorse and guilt about use or behavior when using
• Memory loss, mental confusion, irrational thinking
• Family history of addictive behavior
• Withdrawal discomfort (physical, mental, emotional, and/or psychological)

Courtesy of Roper (1999).

Addiction

There is an urgent need to treat the primary causative factor of the addiction as well as secondary clinical disease as reflected in axial diagnoses: peptic ulcer, avitaminosis, chronic pancreatitis, and so forth (see Section 3.3).

Chronic

Immediate treatment must commence on diagnosis of addiction. Chronic addiction may go into remission. But in the course of treatment, sometimes relapse is inevitable, especially among clients with poor coping skills and/or inconsistent treatment regimes. A prolonged treatment phase is often necessary to achieve long-term sobriety.

Progressive

The progression of addiction is often determined by the choice of psychoactive substance. Addiction can become aggravated rapidly, but with certain drugs such as alcohol, it may be a more gradual progression. Denial and enabling behaviors often facilitate and enhance the progression of addiction.

Terminal

This may stem from major organ destruction, as when cirrhosis of the liver progresses to liver failure and death. This progression is sometimes secondary to chronic alcohol addiction. The risks of contracting hepatitis B, hepatitis C, and human immunodeficiency virus (HIV) are very high. These are highly virulent diseases that could result in loss of life if not adequately managed. Exposure is especially high with intravenous (IV) administration of addictive drugs through contaminated IV needles. This risk could be minimized by supplying sterile needles and syringes to IV drug users called "harm reduction"; it also involves processes of discouraging IV use by supporting safer and less toxic alternative route (for further reading, see Chapter 2). Incidence of fatality due to drug overdose is very prevalent among IV drug users.

Etiology of Addiction

We all have potential for addiction, but specific people may be more predisposed. The causative factors of addiction (chemical dependence) could be intrinsic (genetic) and/or extrinsic (environmental). An interesting aspect is how the interaction between these factors can determine the fate of individuals who struggle with addiction. Before genetics was better understood, genetic predisposition was not considered. The "social judgment call," finger-pointing at individuals or groups, was too common. Today, we are all better informed. Education has provided insight into the science of addiction. The disease of drug addiction is caused by multiple etiological factors. Like diabetes mellitus, it has no set socioeconomic boundaries. However, strong extrinsic causative factors (drug-plagued environments, peer group influence, poor coping skills, post-traumatic stress disorder (PTSD), etc.) often interact with intrinsic (genetic, familial, etc.) conditions, characterizing the demographic of the disease in the population.

The focus of research studies on causes and treatment of drug addiction are subject to continued change as new, more accurate and factual concepts emerge. These studies are the core of discussions in this book with analytical objectivity to attain the ultimate treatment management.

In 1990, the role of genetics in addiction was discovered when researchers unveiled the D2 dopamine receptor (DRD2 gene) and the role it plays in the cause of severe alcoholism. The A1 variance of DRD2 gene was discovered to be involved in addiction susceptibility. This discovery is attributed to the work of Ernest Noble, Professor of Psychiatry and Biobehavioral Sciences and Director of the Alcohol Research Center at the University of California, Los Angeles, and Pharmacologist Kenneth Blum of the University of Texas, San Antonio.

The kinetics of the A1 variance found in a larger percentage of alcoholics, smokers, drug abusers, compulsive or impulsive disorders, and other addictive individuals is manifested in the production of fewer dopamine receptors in the pleasure centers of the brain. Dr. Noble claimed, *"It is only when these individuals with A1 variance abuse drugs and/or alcohol that they feel those pleasures, because the drugs stimulate dopamine production, which in turn stimulates their few dopamine receptors with the result that these individuals begin to feel good. But there is a trap in that, because continued use of the drug causes these individuals to become addicted"* (Werblin, 2011).

Addiction to a particular drug or drugs causes an increased level of dopamine, in spite of fewer dopamine receptors. As such, a compensatory dynamic or "reward (pleasure) deficiency syndrome," in turn causes a need for a higher dose or abuse of the psychoactive drugs to stimulate the pleasure center in A1 variance of DRD2 genes. The compulsion that results from chronic abuse or impulsive use **is the genetic disease** we call addiction.

The team efforts of Noble, Blum, and David E. Comings, MD, Director of the Department of Medical Genetics at City of Hope Medical Center in Duarte, California, stepped up the research and the discovery of polygenetic disorders. According to Dr. Comings, a polygenetic disorder is caused by the additive effect of many genes interacting with the environment. Each gene has only a small effect on the total picture. Different studies find that a single gene of specific addictive substance plays a role, but may not play a role in a group or cluster of multiple addictive substances. It translates that in some groups it is involved and in some groups it is not. That is why researchers believe they need to look at the additive effect of multiple genes to get true picture (Werblin, 2011). This validates the existence of single gene (allele) and polygenic gene variance. These phenotypic presentations are of scientific significance.

Genetic addictive predispositions may also be influenced by environmental interactions: dysfunctional personal behavior or poor coping skills.

The gene MPDZ (involved in influencing physical dependence and withdrawal) was discovered by a team of scientists at Oregon Health & Science University (OHSU) (*Nature Neuroscience 7*, Journal 20 June, 2004). The isolated MPDZ gene is associated with a class of sedative hypnotics widely used to produce euphoric effects. These psychoactive drugs include alcohol, inhalants, barbiturates, benzodiazepines, Rohypnol ("roofies"), and other "club drugs." Keri Buck, PhD, Associate Professor of Behavioral Neuroscience and senior author of the study, confirming a genetic predisposition toward alcoholism and drug addiction, indicates, *"Now that we have identified one of the key genes, we can begin to study how this gene regulates brain circuits involved in drug dependence and withdrawal."*

However, it is paramount to consider other genetic diseases that create vulnerability to addiction. For example, psychotic disorder is a mental illness that defines loss of contact with reality: delusions, illusions, hallucinations (auditory, visual, and olfactory), as well as manic and depressive dysfunction with suicidal ideation, and may to a significant degree be a genetic causative mental disorder. This is not to minimize environmental etiology of mental illness.

Also, extrinsic (environmental) factors are intricately interactive with genetic etiological grounds that determine an additive presentation. However, environmental factors in isolation are just as strong in causative grounds for addiction. These may include social circumstances or peer group pressure along with stress, anxiety, depression, aggression, violence, irritability, and dysfunctional personal behavior (poor coping skills). Post-traumatic stress disorder (PTSD) may be another environmental risk factor. This is an unseen or "invisible wound" that is most devastating especially when it is inflicted in childhood. In general, environmental causative factors carry the same or a relatively fair prognosis compared with genetically induced causative factors in present prevalent psychotherapy procedures. It is frustrating to note that treatment success is less than 50% successful in the overall clinical management process.

The essence of holistic management of addiction is the discovery of its causes and to provide an adequate treatment plan that promotes sobriety and recovery. Because intrinsic causative conditions may be due to genetic variance, this would benefit from complementary pharmacological therapy and psychotherapeutic intervention.

Case Study: Alcoholism in the Family (From Author's Clinical Diary)

Some years ago, when I was a student at the University of Oregon, my favorite spot was the 7/11 store about a block from the University bookstore. One fateful evening about 9 p.m., I stopped by for coffee, my usual stimulant for late-night study.

On my way out to my car, this gentleman drove in and ran his car into my right side (passenger side) front door. After a delayed period and to my shock and surprise, he stepped out of his car, staggering. Every breath reeked with the stench of alcohol. He was a very apologetic middle-aged Caucasian male. He admitted his fault. He appealed to me for a ride home. I agreed to meet him in his office the following day.

His business card indicated he was an ophthalmologist. In his office, he gave me a check for $200, to put it in his words, "For your help of yesterday." He followed up, "...Please, don't let my car insurance agent know about my bad behavior when you contact them for your car repair."

Closeting and denial of his bad habit of alcohol intoxication or most probable case of chronic alcoholism is evident in his statement and attitude.

I warned him to do something about his drinking or he would be in trouble someday. He told me, "My identical twin has the same problem with alcohol." This revelation piqued my curiosity and gave me the idea that alcoholism is sometimes familial or hereditary.

Numerous studies have confirmed that identical genomes as in monozygotic (identical) twins are not absolutely deterministic. Addiction is about 50% intrinsic (genetic) predisposition and approximately 50% extrinsic (environmental, poor coping skills, etc.) conditions—an interactive genome and personal behavior complex.

A study of 861 identical twins and 653 fraternal (nonidentical) twins lends credence to this fact. The nonidentical twins have a low probability of shared alcoholic propensities, but if one identical twin was addicted to alcohol, the other had a 50–60% risk of addiction. This study demonstrates that 50–60% of addiction can be due to genetic factors. The other 40–50% is caused by poor coping skills, where education and information can make a difference. Genetic factors can exert a strong addictive predisposition which can be mitigated by a combined treatment and positive lifestyle. Pure extrinsically induced factors can be strong or feeble depending on multidimensional environmental influences.

Many people come from addicted families but manage to overcome their family history and live happy lives. This opportunity for positive change implies that one's genes are not one's destiny. If someone is determined and committed to a productive life despite genetic inclinations, this motivation provides a basis for psychotherapeutic guidance and redirection.

Another study concluded that children of addicts are eight times more likely to develop an addiction. Thus, aside from genetic predisposition, environmental factors may include negative parental influence, neglect, abuse, childhood exposure to alcohol, and poor lifestyles.

The polygenic theory of addiction is evident in confirmation of cross-addiction. A family history of addiction to a drug could cause addiction to another drug and such a history could result in addiction to any other drug when lifestyles (coping skills) are compromised. On a biomolecular level, studies have shown that multiple genes related to addiction may be involved in similar pathways. This is especially important for women who may come from alcoholic families. These women tend to develop addictions to tranquilizers, pain relievers, or eating disorders.

In a similar genetic complexity, one addiction can lead to other addictions, and one drug can lead to relapse on another as a consequence of a brain wired for addiction. Therefore, if a person is addicted to cocaine and wants to stop using, this individual will have to stop using all addictive or habituating drugs including alcohol and marijuana. While a subject might never have had a problem with either substance, continued use of alcohol or marijuana, even casually, will often lead back to the victim's drug of choice.

For example, clinical detox management of opiate addiction with methadone is indicative of cross-tolerance with other opioids, including heroin and morphine. Methadone is a synthetic opioid used clinically as a maintenance therapy because of its long duration. Other therapeutic effects are as analgesics, anti-viruses, and for the management of chronic pain. However, long-term recovery usually requires total abstinence.

Case Study: Gloria's Drug Abuse (Cross-Addiction) (From Author's Clinical Diary)

In my sophomore class at the University of Oregon, I met a young woman at a nightclub in Eugene. She happened to be a student at the University.

I noticed that on weekends, especially Saturday evenings when she stopped by, her demeanor was often different. She was quiet, an occasional smile but nonconversational. Her blue eyes were pinhole pupil. She appeared withdrawn from the environment and from me.

One Saturday evening when she came by, we had a long talk. She revealed her chronic addiction to heroin and of her family struggle with addiction. Her father was a licensed pilot with a major airline and they used to live in Long Island, New York. He lost his job due to alcohol addiction. Eventually they moved to Springfield, Oregon. Her mom was a registered nurse but she slumped into a deep clinical depression that incapacitated her. While my friend was struggling with heroin addiction, her younger sister's drug of choice was crack cocaine. This woman had never tried alcohol, but her drug of choice was different from her father's; a clinical evidence of cross-addiction.

I supported her decision to register at the school clinic for treatment, encouraged her to attend the treatment sessions, and sometimes accompanied her to support groups.

This case of family addiction demonstrates cross-addiction: parental alcoholism and depression leading to siblings' different choices of addictive drugs and poor coping skills. It is a vicious cycle that ensures generational addiction. It is evident that a family history of addiction can be a recipe for vulnerability to variety of addictions in all family members. Addiction is a dangerous and life-threatening disease. Therefore, it is imperative that we continue to study addictive behaviors and how they manifest in families through genetics and environment, and to continue to apply a variety of therapies in an ongoing effort to break the cycle of addiction.

2 Common Psychoactive Drugs

In this chapter, we shall discuss common psychoactive drugs and their properties and effects, as these drugs can have serious consequences on an abuser, addict, family, friends, and others, devastating behavioral dysfunctions and even death.

The various psychoactive drugs include stimulants, depressants, hallucinogens, and so on. The impact on the central nervous system (CNS) is related to their mechanisms of action. The polydrug or multiple drug culture often encouraged in our society can promote indiscriminate use of mixtures of these classes of drugs that may enhance and exacerbate toxic effect, sometimes increasing fatality risks.

The following list is only a partial list of all known drugs in their respective categories. We will examine a few from each category.

CNS stimulants
    Cocaine
    Amphetamines
    Caffeine
    Nicotine.
CNS depressants and hypnotics
    Alcohol
    Benzodiazepines
    Barbiturates.
Opioids
    Heroin
    Other opium derivatives, morphine.
CNS hallucinogens
    LSD
    Phencyclidine
    MDMA
    Other related hallucinogens.

2.1 Alcohol

Alcohol is an organic compound in which a hydroxyl functional group (OH) is bound to a carbon atom. The carbon atom is further bounded to hydrogen(s) and other carbon atom(s). A partial oxidation of alcohol is an aldehyde, while a complete oxidation is a carboxylic acid. For example, methyl alcohol (wood alcohol) is a highly dangerous form of alcohol found in household products such as antifreeze, fuel, and paint thinner. Rubbing alcohol is a mixture usually consisting of 70%

Practical Skills and Clinical Management of Alcoholism and Drug Addiction.
DOI: http://dx.doi.org/10.1016/B978-0-12-398518-7.00002-X

isopropyl or absolute alcohol, applied externally to disinfect or soothe skin as well as relieve muscle and joint pain.

Some common street names of alcohol are booze, brew, cold one, juice, sauce, vino, hard stuff, and so forth. Alcohol is measured by "proof." Proof is a term that quantifies the amount of alcohol found in various liquor products. The "proof" number denotes double the percentage of alcohol found in the product. For example, Everclear is 90% proof alcohol which means it contains 45% alcohol.

The disease of alcoholism is an excessive consumption of alcoholic beverages that interfere with physical, physiological, and mental health as well as social, family, or job responsibilities and commitments. When tolerance to intake and withdrawal symptoms are observed, addiction is defined.

Alcohol has a depressant effect on the nervous system. It causes a decrease in activity, anxiety, inhibition, tension, and impairment of judgment and concentration. Other signs and symptoms include episodes of violence while drinking, denial coupled with hostility when confronted, malnutrition from neglect, shaking in the morning, and a demand for early morning alcohol intake to function. Alcohol withdrawal symptoms include anxiety, hallucinations, increased blood pressure, loss of appetite, nausea/or vomiting, or death.

Blood Alcohol Level/Concentration

One standard drink equals 5 ounces of wine; 12 ounces of beer; or 1.5 ounces of 80 proof distilled spirits (Table 2.1).

The blood alcohol concentration limits range between 0.08 and 0.10, according to various state laws.

We have a great deal of knowledge about the insidious onset of alcoholism. In spite of clear signs and symptoms, it is critical to establish a line between social and problem drinking. This can most often be determined through examination in significant depth into troubling behaviors (Table 2.2).

Women and Alcohol

It is evident that women are more sensitive to alcohol than men. Women have a lower average weight and a higher concentration of alcohol in the body fluid with identical doses of alcohol being administered. But many factors beyond size and weight play a part in the state of sensitivity of either gender: type and proof of alcohol, consumption rate, amount of food ingested, and interactions with other psychoactive drugs. Another intervening factor may be less production of alcohol dehydrogenase in women.

Although the consumption of alcohol with water may slow down the absorption rate, it usually takes approximately 1 h to metabolize one drink. Postalcohol consumption hangover is resolved over time when the body restores itself subject to natural body mechanisms.

Women are also more vulnerable to adverse consequences of alcohol use: liver and brain damage, heart disease, violent victimization, and road traffic accidents. Alcohol acts as a physiological depressant of libido in women.

Table 2.1 Amount of Alcohol in the Blood

Weight (lb)	Drinks									
	1	2	3	4	5	6	7	8	9	10
Men										
100	0.04	0.08	0.11	0.15	0.19	0.23	0.26	0.30	0.34	0.38
120	0.03	0.06	0.09	0.12	0.16	0.19	0.22	0.25	0.28	0.31
140	0.03	0.05	0.08	0.11	0.13	0.16	0.19	0.21	0.24	0.27
160	0.02	0.05	0.07	0.09	0.12	0.14	0.16	0.19	0.21	0.23
180	0.02	0.04	0.06	0.08	0.11	0.13	0.15	0.17	0.19	0.21
200	0.02	0.04	0.06	0.08	0.09	0.11	0.13	0.15	0.17	0.19
220	0.02	0.03	0.05	0.07	0.09	0.10	0.12	0.14	0.15	0.17
240	0.02	0.03	0.05	0.06	0.08	0.09	0.11	0.13	0.14	0.16
Women										
100	0.05	0.09	0.14	0.18	0.23	0.27	0.32	0.36	0.41	0.45
120	0.04	0.08	0.11	0.15	0.19	0.23	0.27	0.30	0.34	0.38
140	0.03	0.07	0.10	0.13	0.16	0.18	0.23	0.26	0.29	0.32
160	0.03	0.06	0.09	0.11	0.14	0.17	0.20	0.23	0.26	0.28
180	0.03	0.05	0.08	0.10	0.13	0.15	0.18	0.20	0.23	0.25
200	0.02	0.05	0.07	0.09	0.11	0.14	0.16	0.18	0.20	0.23
220	0.02	0.04	0.06	0.08	0.10	0.12	0.14	0.17	0.19	0.21
240	0.02	0.04	0.06	0.08	0.09	0.11	0.13	0.15	0.17	0.19

Source: Courtesy of Storie (2005).

Table 2.2 Effect of Excessive Alcohol Consumption

Short-Term Physiological Effects	Short-Term Psychological Effects	
Incoordination	Delusions	Aggressive humor
Slurred speech	Loss of memory	Impaired judgment
Staggering	Loss of control	Decreased inhibition
Elevated heartbeat	Irritability	Alteration of sensation
Increased urine output	Euphoria	Inability to predict outcome
Drowsiness	Hostility	Increased risk-taking behavior
	Confusion	Alteration of perception
	Paranoia	

Source: Courtesy of Storie (2005).

A study of drinking behavior involving a sample of female twins was meant to identify significant environmental factors. Those who managed this study concluded that, *"Among women, marital status appears to modify the effects of genetic factors that influence drinking habits. Marriage or marriage-like relationships interfere with and lessen the effect of an inherited liability for drinking"* (Heath and colleagues (8)).

Various researchers have reported drinking patterns and alcohol-related problems among women of different racial and ethnic groups: Black women (46%) are more likely to abstain from alcohol than white women (34%). Many complex factors, including age, siblings, marital status, social status, and peer groups, can play significant roles as unpredictable variables which may impact an inclination toward addiction.

As with any alcoholic behavior, women's chronic alcoholism may progress to late-stage complications of liver and pancreatic damage, malnutrition, avitaminosis, and hypertension, at a faster rate without intervention.

A research study recently done at the Harvard School of Public Health and a Harvard-affiliated hospital confirms the relationship between alcohol and depression. Analysis of the data revealed that having a greater number of symptoms of alcoholism significantly increased the risk of developing depression. Women are two to seven times more at risk than men for developing depression. In other words, these results mean that women are more likely to be diagnosed with both disorders at the same time compared to men. The implications of this study are important, as it verifies the relationship between depression and alcohol as quite strong, especially among women.

Drug addiction and/or alcoholism during pregnancy often may cause severe brain damage in the newborn. Fetal alcohol syndrome refers to growth, mental, and physical problems from excessive alcohol use during pregnancy (especially in the first trimester). Abnormal growth features microcephaly (small head), decreased muscle tone with poor coordination, and delayed developmental milestones in thinking, speech, movement, and social skills. Cardiovascular system complications include congenital ventricular septal defect and/or atrial septal defect. This manifests as retardation throughout the life of the baby.

Breast cancer has been confirmed to be a significant risk factor of alcohol consumption. In May 2000, alcoholic beverages were listed as a known carcinogen by the US Department of Health and Human Services (for further reading, see Section 5.4).

2.2   Impact of High-Risk Drinking

Social, legal, medical, domestic, and financial problems are caused by perennial high-risk drinking, while drunkenness behind the wheel most often results in fatal accidents (Figure 2.1).

Chronic alcoholism is often associated with poor nutrition, inflammation of the esophagus and stomach, which progresses to ulceration of these viscera. Chronic pancreatitis is another inflammatory process caused by chronic alcoholism. This condition may present with ascites, abdominal pain, pale or clay-colored stools, and weight loss. This often leads to disability or death.

Deficiency of thiamin (Vitamin B1) as a result of chronic compromised nutrition due to chronic alcoholism that precipitates serious brain damage was discovered by a Polish neurologist, Dr. Carl Wernicke, in 1881. Wernicke encephalopathy is a triad of acute mental confusion, ataxia (loss of voluntary muscular movement coordination), and ophthalmoplegia (eye muscle(s) paralysis). Korsakoff amnesic syndrome describes a late clinical manifestation of Wernicke encephalopathy with memory loss

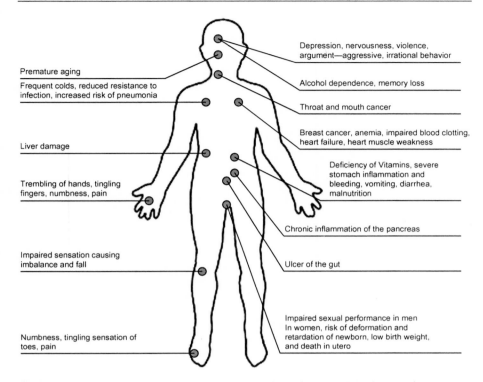

Depression, nervousness, violence, argument—aggressive, irrational behavior

Premature aging

Frequent colds, reduced resistance to infection, increased risk of pneumonia

Alcohol dependence, memory loss

Throat and mouth cancer

Breast cancer, anemia, impaired blood clotting, heart failure, heart muscle weakness

Liver damage

Deficiency of Vitamins, severe stomach inflammation and bleeding, vomiting, diarrhea, malnutrition

Trembling of hands, tingling fingers, numbness, pain

Chronic inflammation of the pancreas

Impaired sensation causing imbalance and fall

Ulcer of the gut

Impaired sexual performance in men In women, risk of deformation and retardation of newborn, low birth weight, and death in utero

Numbness, tingling sensation of toes, pain

Figure 2.1 Besides a plethora of systemic compromise, seizures and death are serious complications of acute or chronic alcoholism. Detoxification of alcohol takes place in the liver. A chronic, excessive intake with loss of appetite that compromises nutritional health could lead to liver cirrhosis, liver fattening, and abnormal redistribution of fats over the body, especially around the stomach. It is not surprising to see a male alcoholic with an extended abdomen (6-month pregnancy size) due to fats and excessive abdominal fluid retention (ascites). Also present may be added liver and pancreatic enlargement due to this inflammatory process. Bilateral hand tremor is one of the clinical signs of liver disease, a pointer to alcoholism as a significant differential diagnosis.

and confabulation. Confabulation is clinical defective recall of events by a patient or client diagnosed with Wernicke–Korsakoff syndrome psychosis. This memory disorder is related to amnesia and involves fabricated accounts of events, either deliberate or without conscious intent, to compensate for memory loss. This behavior is sometimes referred to as "honest lying."

Although alcohol abuse can lead to chronic alcoholism and death, an appropriate amount of alcohol may have some health benefits. Two drinks a day for men and one drink a day for women (considering a standard drink as a value of 5 ounces of wine; 12 ounces of beer, or 1.5 ounces of 80 proof distilled spirits) are the optimum quantities for enhancing lower mortality rates. At this healthy dose of one to two drinks a day, alcohol is a mild antioxidant. At this level, the drug has a capability to neutralize detrimental and possibly carcinogenic free oxygen radicals produced during systemic biochemical reactions. This antioxidant property reduces the risks of cancer and atherosclerotic heart disease. Moderate alcohol consumption may also reduce risks of myocardial infarction caused by atherosclerotic lesions of cardiac blood vessels.

The mechanism of action is the alteration of the good/bad cholesterol ratio in a healthy direction. It is essential to consider the appropriate dose in order to maximize these benefits. It must be emphasized that alcoholic beverages are not the only sources for these benefits. The vitamin C in oranges, grapes, blueberries, and blackberries (coupled with a healthy lifestyle) are alternatives.

Case Study: From a DUI Group Counseling Session (From Author's Clinical Diary)

Clinical case report: I conducted a group counseling session of some clients convicted of DUI (driving under the influence of alcohol). This is a mandatory course administered by the state. In the middle of an interaction, one client informed the group, "This is my first DUI ticket. And after today's session, I'll be okay to have my license back." I responded by validating his feelings for attending all his required sessions. I added, "This is also a period for a moment of self-search for the cause of the intoxication. The ticket is a consequence of a behavior which may be secondary to recurrent alcohol abuse." I described the etiologies of addiction: familial depression, PTSD, genetic-induced addiction, psychiatric illness, etc. By the conclusion of my admonition, he admitted to a family history of intense depression. He claimed he frequently medicated with alcohol to alleviate periodic depressive moments. Because of the limited session time, he requested a referral for treatment. This case represents a classic case of denial. The client was prepared to get back behind the steering wheel and become a danger to himself and others. But the intervention served as a tipping point for awareness and self-acceptance of objective reality. This most probably elicits an insight that facilitates a commitment to medical treatment. Counseling/psychotherapy often sows and nurtures the seed of mental (cognitive) wellness. The beauty as well as the frustration of the process is the prognosis attained through the procedure. Ultimately, this is a function of individual commitment to treatment, vulnerability, and severity of the disease.

2.3 Cocaine

Simply known as coke, cocaine is an alkaloid obtained from the leaves of coca plants commonly found in South America. Street names include: flake, snow, toot, blow, nose candy, her, she, lady flack, liquid lady (alcohol + cocaine), speedball (cocaine + heroin), crack, rock, and other variations.

Cocaine is a powerful CNS stimulant. Its effect could last from 15 min to an hour, depending on route of administration. As a stimulant, cocaine enhances alertness and alters perceptions regarding physical capabilities, athletic performance, and sexuality. While users may experience euphoria, behavioral symptoms of cocaine use may include anxiety, paranoia, and restlessness.

The naming expresses the appearance, use, and contents of the mixture. At present, cocaine is the most abused stimulant in America because of its powerful psychologically addictive properties. The drug also acts as an analgesic and appetite suppressant. It specifically inhibits the reuptake of serotonin–norepinephrine–dopamine, which as an exogenous catecholamine transporter enhances the mesolimbic reward pathway and is responsible for cocaine's profound addictive properties.

In 1885, before prohibition, US manufacturer Parke-Davis sold cocaine in different forms as cigarettes, powder, and mixtures. It was overtly sold as cocaine or in mixtures with alcohol or heroin, along with IV needles for injection. Companies commercialized cocaine, with their knowledge of its properties and actions, as a product that could *"supply the place of food, make the coward brave, silent the eloquent, and render the sufferer insensitive to pain."*

In 1886, a "brain tonic" (a combination of cocaine from coca leaves and caffeine from the African kola nut) was named Coca Cola Elixir and mainly sold in Atlanta. It was then recommended for the treatment of headaches, alcoholism, morphine addiction, abdominal pain, and menstrual cramps. By 1914, cocaine became a strictly controlled drug. It was labeled as a narcotic and considered dangerous.

The usual pattern of drug abuse in the United States is a form of multiple or polydrug abuse. This often entails a combination with other drugs that moderate the side effects of the primary drug, as with an upper or downer counteracting or complementing one another. Cocaine is usually combined with sedatives such as alcohol, Valium, Ativan, or heroin. The most common cocaine mixture is with alcohol and marijuana.

The extract from the leaves of the coca plant is a crystalline tropane alkaloid called cocaine ($C_{17}H_{21}NO_4$). It is converted to a white salt, cocaine hydrochloride ($C_{17}H_{21}NO_4 \cdot HCl$) in a clandestine lab in South America before its transportation through all routes to the streets of the United States, and this salt form is the purest, as much as 95% pure cocaine. The street market purity ranges from 95% to 1% because of adulteration processes which may include baking soda, sugars, mannitol, dextrose, lactose, inositol, and local anesthetics such as lidocaine or benzocaine. It is also "cut" or "stepped on" with other stimulants like methamphetamine. It is water soluble in this form. Thus, its route of administration includes the following:

Insufflation: Also known as "snorting," "sniffing," or "blowing." In this process, the drug is absorbed through the mucus membrane at a 30–60% rate. The rest is collected in mucus and swallowed. It takes an average of 14.6 min to reach a peak subjective effect. Sharing of straws to "snort" cocaine could spread blood-borne diseases such as Hepatitis C.

Injection: IV administration attains a peak subjective effect in 3.1 min. When in excess of 120 mg, it causes tinnitus (a ringing in the ear) which lasts about 2–5 min. This is often locally referred to as a "bell ringer." Among the detrimental effects are the circulatory emboli that could be precipitated by the presence of insoluble substance employed to "cut" the drug. Fatal complications such as pulmonary embolism and stroke are possible outcomes. Shared needles might result in the spread of Hepatitis B, C, HIV, and other blood diseases.

A toxic combination of cocaine and other drugs such as heroin may counteract possible symptoms of overdose, but still lead to death (Table 2.3).

Table 2.3 Effect of Cocaine Consumption

Short-Term Physiological Effects	Short-Term Psychological Effects
Increased heart rate	Euphoria
Increased blood pressure	Excitation
Runny nose	Restlessness
Muscle twitching	Anxiety
Sexual stimulation	Increased arousal
Insomnia	Increased alertness
Loss of appetite	Irritability
Increase in motor activity	Auditory hallucinations
Increase in rate of speech	Delusions
Dilated pupils	Paranoia
Elevated temperature	Perceived increase in strength
Sweating	Feelings of enhanced mental ability
Dry mouth	
Seizures	
Sudden cardiac arrest	

Source: Courtesy of Storie (2005).

Inhalation: Freebase or crack cocaine is the solid, insoluble form of cocaine. It is produced by heating coke and highly volatile ether to form cocaine sulfate. Crack (cloud nine) is extracted with relative lower heating of a combination of coke and baking soda that forms rock-like pieces. Crack cocaine is a lower purity form of freebase cocaine that contains impurities such as sodium bicarbonate. These impurities are responsible for the crackling sound when the substance is heated and smoked. The heat causes sublimation, which is inhaled. The subjective "peak high" occurs within 1.4 min. Crack, when smoked, is sometimes combined with other drugs such as cannabis and is sometimes sprinkled on marijuana (cannabis), evidence of polydrug use.

Behavioral interventions, particularly cognitive-behavioral therapy (CBT), have been shown to be effective in decreasing use and preventing relapse. Treatment must be accommodated to individual needs to optimize outcomes. This often may include a combination of treatments, social supports, and other services. Currently, there are no Food and Drug Administration (FDA)-approved medications for treating cocaine addiction.

2.4 Cannabis

Also known as marijuana, ganja, or hemp, cannabis is the most common illicit drug abused in the United States. Mixtures of its leaves, stems, flowers, and seeds are derived from the hemp plant, *Cannabis sativa*. The primary active chemical in marijuana is a delta-9-tetrahydrocannabinol, abbreviated as THC.

The *route of administration* is commonly by inhalation via smoking. Sometimes, the substance may be mixed with tobacco, cocaine, and other drugs. Marijuana may be ingested with food or brewed as tea.

Table 2.4 Effect of Marijuana Consumption

Short-Term Physiological Effects	Short-Term Psychological Effects
Dry mouth	Euphoria
Increased blood pressure	Relaxation
Increased heart rate	Disturbance in short-term memory
Involuntary movements	Altered perception of time and space
Impaired coordination	Impaired judgment
Headaches	Increased reaction time
Numbness	Confusion
Dizziness	Paranoia
Increased appetite	Mild anxiety
Tremors	Detachment from reality
Drowsiness	Hallucinations
Blood vessels in eyes expand, resulting in red eyes	Heightened sensitivity to sound, sight, taste, and emotionality
Decrease in REM sleep	
Mild slowing in alpha-wave frequency	
Sedation	
Impaired critical thinking skills (up to 24 h)	
Increased sexual arousal	

Source: Courtesy of Storie (2005).

Hashish has a higher concentration of THC than marijuana (ranging from 5% to 20%). The processed marijuana produces a sticky resin and is most potent when extracted from female cannabis plants. Extraction of THC directly from the cannabis plant in liquid form results in hashish oil. The THC concentration of the oil may exceed 30%.

Effects on the Brain: In the process of smoking marijuana, THC is absorbed through the lungs into the blood and then permeates the blood–brain barrier to be introduced into the brain. THC specifically acts on cannabinoid receptors concentrated at various brain centers including the hippocampus, basal ganglia, and cerebellum. These receptors modulate pleasure, memory, thoughts, concentration, sensory and time perception, and movement coordination.

The interaction between THC and the receptors triggers a cascade of reactions that result in a "pleasure" feeling at the dopamine release center, nucleus accumbens. Marijuana use results in this "high," along with impairment of mental functions of other affected brain centers. Excessive use that results in intoxication can cause distorted perceptions, coordination impairment, disturbed thinking, problems with processing and resolving, and problems with learning and memory. This brain function compromise could last for fairly long periods, even after the drug effect has subsided.

A daily dose of marijuana might precipitate suboptimal intellectual function during the time of use. Long-term use might cause neuronal damage especially in dopamine neuron cells, which often modulate motivation and pleasure activities. This is usually the vulnerable neuron complex targeted directly or indirectly by all drugs of abuse (Table 2.4).

Addiction may result from long-term use of marijuana. Withdrawal symptoms include irritability, sleeplessness, decreased appetite, anxiety, and drug craving. Symptoms peak at 2–3 days and subside within 1–2 weeks after quitting.

Mental Illness: Chronic use of marijuana has been associated with risk factors of mental illness. This may result in the onset or relapse of schizophrenia in vulnerable clients. High doses could produce an acute psychotic reaction.

Effects on the Heart: The systemic effects after smoking include increased heart rate by 20–100%. It could be complicated by change in rhythm, resulting in palpitation and arrhythmias. This is particularly a high risk among aging clients with preexisting cardiac pathology.

Effects on Lungs: Marijuana contains more irritants and carcinogenic hydrocarbons (50–70%) than tobacco. Ironically, it is not commonly associated with causing cancer. Studies have demonstrated that respiratory illnesses are far more common with marijuana versus tobacco smokers.

Metabolism: THC is stored in body fats after consumption. There is a prolonged effect after the last dose administered. This effect might last 5 days or more after the last dose because up to 20% of the THC is retained in body fat. It could take approximately 30 days to completely eliminate the dose from the body. THC metabolism primarily takes place in the liver by the cytochrome p450 enzymes. Over 55% is excreted in the feces and about 29% via urine.

Therapeutic Uses: THC has a mild-to-moderate analgesic effect. It restores appetite. It is claimed to have a relaxation and antiemetic effect. These functions of pain, nausea, and vomiting relief, stimulation of appetite, induced relaxation, and euphoria are essential properties and medically beneficial in the symptomatic management of chronic and terminal illnesses such as cancer, acquired immunodeficiency syndrome (AIDS), glaucoma, multiple sclerosis, neuropathic pain, and spasticity. Fourteen states, including Oregon, Washington, and California, have enacted laws that legalize "medical marijuana."

Active Compounds (Cannabinoids) in Marijuana

Three types of cannabinoids are as follows:

1. Endo-cannabinoids
2. Phyto-cannabinoids
3. Syntho-cannabinoids (synthetic cannabis).

Endo-cannabinoids are natural chemicals made inside the human body. They are omnipresent and essential to biologic functions of the body. They are derivatives of arachidonic acid conjugated with ethanolamine or glycerol which resemble other lipid transmitters such as eicosanoids (prostaglandins or leucotrienes). The endogenous cannabinoid system is a lipid-signaling system that performs important regulatory functions throughout the body. Its ubiquity and evolutionary presence is of utmost essence in vertebrates.

They bind to natural cannabinoid CB1 receptors which are heavily distributed in brain areas related to motor control, cognition, emotional responses, motivated behavior, and homeostasis. The endogenous cannabinoid system also functions as modulators of the autonomic nervous system (ANS), immune system, and microcirculation.

Phyto-cannabinoids are natural chemicals made inside plants. The two active compounds are THC and cannabidiol (CBD). THC is a CB1, CB2 receptor agonist and the primary psychoactive ingredient. The biologic activities of CBD are CB1, CB2 receptor antagonist, significant analgesic and anti-inflammatory actions without the psychoactive effect (High) of THC.

There are three types of cannabis: Ruderalis (least THC), Indica, and Sativa (both containing approximately same THC—1% THC:1% CBD). It is believed that Sativa is indigenous to the Americas, while Indica was imported to America by Europeans for cloth, paper, canvas, and so on.

Synthetic Cannabis: K2 and Spice are brand names of synthetic cannabis, a psychoactive herbal and chemical product which when consumed mimic the effect of cannabis. These brand names have largely become generic trademarks used to refer to any synthetic cannabis products. Syntho-cannabinoids are man-made synthetic or semisynthetic chemicals. Synthetic cannabinoids act on the body in a similar way to cannabinoids naturally found in cannabis such as THC. It appears as a large and complex variety of synthetic cannabinoids, most often cannabicyclohexanol, JWH-018, JWH-073, or HU-210.

The users of synthetic cannabis are attracted to this psychoactive drug because of its high potency. This designer drug does not produce positive results in a drug test for cannabis but its metabolic products in human urine are detectable.

The manipulative process which involves the environmental condition or genetic reconstruction enhances increased psychoactive chemical (THC) production of cannabis. For example, the Sinsemilla technique involves creating an artificial condition by restricting pollination. Hydroponics and cloning in the 1980s favored an artificial environment. Selective pollination of 1982 promoted diploid to polyploidy, enhancing genetic manipulation. Halide lights of the 1980s substituted natural sunlight with artificial sunlight up to 24 h/day. Also, carbon dioxide gas of the 1990s provided artificial atmosphere.

A study conducted at University of Mississippi revealed a lineal increment of THC potency in marijuana due to growth manipulation, from 1974 to 2008 at a range from 1% to about 10%. Presently, man-made marijuana has been produced with 37.2% THC and 1–5% CBD. The product is whitish in appearance compared to natural marijuana of 1% THC and 1% CBD of vegetable-green coloration. As the strong dopaminergic effect of psychogenic THC increases with increased THC potency, it enhances euphoria and high probability of psychosis on abuse/addiction.

Synthetic cannabis is often marketed under various brand names such as "herbal incense" and "herbal smoking blends." Either of the brands is smoked by users. These products are commercialized and sold online, in head shops, and at some gas stations.

As of March 1, 2011, US Drug Enforcement Agency has declared five cannabinoids Schedule 1 drugs, JWH-018, JWH-073, CP-47,497, JWH-200, and cannabicyclohexanol, illegal in the United States.

Sativex is cannabis extract 1:1THC:CBD. It is an oromucosal spray approved in Canada for adjunctive treatment of pain due to multiple sclerosis neuropathy and cancer.

2.5 Amphetamines

Amphetamines belong to Class B prescription drugs under the Medicine Act and the Misuse of Drugs Act of 1971. These are legally prescribed by doctors and unauthorized possession constitutes an offense. These drugs are categorized under Schedule II along with cocaine. They are synthetic stimulants of the CNS. They are known as uppers, bennies, beans, speed, and crank. They bear structural and functional similarities to natural neurotransmitters such as adrenaline produced in the body in fight or flight emergencies.

Amphetamines are sympathomimetic agents with bronchodilator properties. The three main types are amphetamine sulfate, commonly referred to as speed with a trade name—Benzedrine (copilot), dextroamphetamine (Dexedrine or "Dexy's Midnight Runners"), and methamphetamine as Methedrine or "Meth," which is the most potent.

The chemical properties and actions of these substances are so similar that experienced users of amphetamine derivatives found it difficult to separate differential psychoactive effects.

Amphetamine does have clinical uses but abuse and consequent addiction become apparent with an increase in medical use. Truckers too often indiscriminately use the drug without a physician's recommendation and guidelines. Amphetamine use can facilitate completion of long routes without falling asleep. The drug may be used for weight control, to help athletes to perform better and train longer, and for self-management of depression.

Clinical Application: The FDA has approved dextroamphetamine and methylphenidate for therapy in the treatment of narcolepsy and attention-deficit hyperactivity disorder (ADHD). Appetite inhibitors such as fenfluramine and chlorpheniramine are the effective weight-control agents found in amphetamines. Other symptoms that respond to stimulants are anhedonia (the inability to feel pleasure), lack of energy, easy fatigue, and low self-esteem. Specific examples may include dysthymic disorders and "atypical depression" associated with medical illness (i.e., poststroke depression) and HIV neuropsychiatric symptoms.

Methamphetamine: Ice, also known as "crystal meth," is generally referred to as freebase methamphetamine. This is a form of amphetamine that can be smoked and is similar in preparation to "freebasing" cocaine. It comes in a larger crystal or rocks. Inhalation from smoking enhances rapid and large dosage absorption into the blood. This promotes a higher peak and increased neurotoxicity within the shortest time, analogous to cocaine inhalation via smoking, but with a longer duration. Ice has the highest potency as compared with other forms of amphetamines.

Amphetamines: Speed, also referred to as black beauties, pink hearts, and diet pills, can be taken orally or injected. These stimulants decrease the need for sleep and food and produce feelings similar to those associated with cocaine.

High dosages can result in rapid and irregular heartbeat, tremors, loss of coordination, and physical collapse. Moderate dosages precipitate dry mouth, fever, sweating, headache, blurred vision, dizziness, diarrhea, and loss of appetite. Low dosages cause increased breathing, faster heart rate, higher blood pressure, and dilated pupils. Sudden death due to stroke, fever, and heart failure can be caused by injection.

Overdose could present symptoms including restlessness, tremors, rapid breathing, confusion, hallucinations, panic, aggressiveness, nausea, vomiting, diarrhea, seizures, and irregular heartbeat.

Withdrawal symptoms are depression, stomach cramps, nausea, or vomiting, "the shakes," and tiredness. These are generic reactions to all the amphetamine derivatives according to their relative toxicity and the timing of the withdrawal process.

2.6 Sedatives, Hypnotics, and Anxiolytics

These are activities of barbiturates and diazepines. Action involves increased GABA activity (an inhibitory neurotransmitter in the brain stem), including sleep and depressing the muscular system.

Phenobarbital is rarely abused because of its slow onset of action and high margin of safety relative to other psychoactive drugs. It is often used to detoxify people from physical dependencies on other sedatives because of its low abuse liability that entails a long duration of action and safety.

Examples are barbital or Amytal, pentobarbital, Nembutal, secobarbital (seconal), methaqualone (Quaaludes/"ludes"), Valium, and Librium. Methods of administration are oral or IV ingestion. Most of these drugs are medications controlled under the Physician Prescription Act and they may be used to induce sleep. Anxiolytics are known to reduce anxiety. Long-term use of prescribed sedatives could cause habituation, a state when a patient is accustomed to prescription of sedative and feels it is impossible to sleep without it. Habituation is often confused with physical dependence.

Abuse may also be a complication of prescribed medical use. These drugs may expose a high growing class of medicine users or just the usual street drug users' entertainment, to addiction from frequent "pleasurable trips." Thus, abuse can cause problems with concentration, speech, judgment, mood, sexuality, and impulses.

Quaaludes ("ludes") could cause dry mouth, headaches, dizziness, chills, and diarrhea. Overdose could precipitate delirium, convulsions, and death, especially in cases of multiple drug use such as a regimen of alcohol, barbiturate, or benzodiazepine that potentiate sedative effect and result in depression of the respiratory center. Valium and other benzodiazepine can cause hostile or aggressive behavior, nausea, sweating, and convulsions.

2.7 Hallucinogens

Drugs and street names of hallucinogens include LSD (angel tears, battery acid), phencyclidine (PCP, angel, amoeba, butt naked), and MDMA (clarity).

LSD

Most potent hallucinogens are extracted from fungus or mold and rye bread. Transportation is facilitated by impregnating the psychoactive chemical on the gummy side of a stamp, sticker, or envelope because of its colorless, odorless, and tasteless properties.

Administration: Orally in a paper, gel, or capsule form called "microdots" or blotter paper or as liquid (angel tears).

Action: Hallucinogens stimulate serotonin receptors in the brain for a long duration. These receptors are concentrated in the hypothalamus, limbic system, auditory, and visual areas, resulting in alterations in perception. This type of drug activates the sympathetic nervous system and parasympathetic nervous system which modulate temperature and salivation. Metabolism takes place in the liver and these substances are excreted through the small intestine.

A bad "trip" is a characteristic experience that results in extreme fear, panic, depression, or anxiety that mimic a schizophrenic-like episode. When taking hallucinogens such as LSD, a panic attack can develop which may cause a subject to jump out of a window, suddenly jump into the pathway of a running vehicle, or take some other rash action causing serious injury.

Long-term visual hallucinations are also characteristic: flashbacks which occur long after the use. There is a high risk of developing psychological dependence due to the intense euphoria experienced during a trip.

Phencyclidine

Phencyclidine (also known as PCP, angel, amoeba, butt naked) is clinically a very effective anesthetic because it does not cause depression of the respiratory and cardiovascular centers, but it may have an effect which mimics psychotic episodes. Drug users employ it for its hallucinogenic and euphoric effects. It is also a stimulant, depressant, analgesic, and anesthetic. It is smoked or snorted, taken orally in pill form, or mixed with liquid and injected. Actions involve stimulating glutamate receptors, an excitatory neurotransmitter. It is fat soluble and its intermittent release affects the hallucinogenic and euphoric properties.

In multiple drug use, PCP may commonly be dusted on tobacco or marijuana and smoked, a combination referred to as "angel dust." A combination of PCP, heroin, and alcohol could cause intense psychoactive effects and fatality.

MDMA

MDMA (also known as ecstasy), a synthetic psychoactive chemical, is a combination of amphetamine and LSD. This substance acts as a stimulant and has psychedelic effects. It is mainly administered orally, but could also be smoked or snorted.

Action: In a mild dose, ecstasy causes increase in the release of dopamine and norepinephrine. In a higher dose, MDMA acts as a serotonin agonist, causing an increase in serotonin release and blocking its uptake. This activity is responsible for the hallucinations produced by MDMA. There may be psychological dependence due to intense euphoria, but no evidence has established physical dependency.

Other Hallucinogens

Mescaline is psychoactive drug naturally occurring in peyote. This is often used as a legal drug by Native American church members for religious ceremonies. It is about 2000 times less potent than LSD.

Psilocybin: This is more potent than mescaline, and naturally occurs in *Psilocybe mexicana* mushrooms.

DMT is a short-acting hallucinogen which is synthesized and also naturally occurs in seeds of leguminous trees in the West Indies and South America. Its duration is about 1 h, similar to psilocybin.

2.8 Opioids

These are naturally occurring psychoactive drugs derived from the opium poppy (*Papaver somniferum*) or synthetic derivates of opium and its families. It is unique to note that most of the synthetics and some naturally occurring ones are primarily processed for medicinal purposes (Figure 2.2).

LAAM

Levo-alpha acetyl methadol (LAAM) is a medication therapy for individuals addicted to opiates that provides an alternative to methadone. It is advantageous

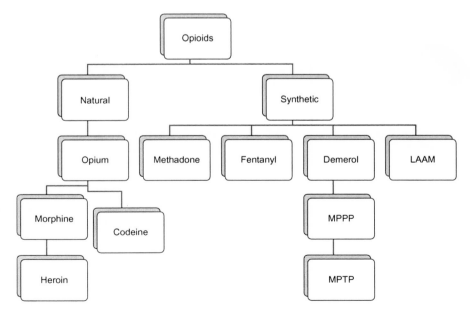

Figure 2.2 Opioids.
Source: Courtesy of Storie (2005).

because of its longer life span when given to heroin-dependent patients in treatment. It is administered three times a week, thus the convenience of fewer trips to the hospital. It acts by blocking the opiate receptor sites, preventing the effect of other opiates, and it has no withdrawal effect. LAAM has no "subjective high." For further discussion, see LAAM in Pharmacotherapy (Section 6.2).

- MPPP—1-methyl-4-phenyl 4-propionoxypiperidine
- MPTP—1-methyl-4-phenyl-1,2,3,6-tetrahydropyridine.

These two related synthetic narcotics are most often injected and carry risks of association with the development of permanent parkinsonism. This may result in tremors, muscle rigidity, shuffling gait, slow speech, and mask-like facial expressions. Use of these synthetics may be complicated by analgesia, catatonia, respiratory depression, and the loss of sight and cornea reflexes.

Morphine is extracted from opium as a black or dark brown sap. This narcotic is unique, highly potent, and characterized by speed and degree of affectivity when administered orally. This extract is used medically for treatment of pain, anxiety, and depression. The drug has a sedative effect and propensity for respiratory depression. The use of this drug may cause constipation (antidiarrhea), pupillary constriction, and lower blood pressure.

Heroin

Diacetylmorphine, also known as smack, H, skag, junk, is a semisynthetic opioid drug designed from morphine, a natural derivative of opium poppy (*Papaver somniferum*). The white crystalline form is commonly its hydrochloride salt. This form is often adulterated into white, white pale, or brown powder.

History: Diacetylmorphine was first synthesized by C.R. Alder, an English chemist at St. Mary's Hospital Medical School in London in 1874. His goal and aspiration was to design a nonaddictive form of opium that retained its highly effective pain-relieving properties. The ideal expectation was not achieved. Diacetylmorphine retained both addictive and pain-relieving properties. Twenty-three years later, in Elberfeld Germany, a chemist named Felix Hoffmann on Bayer Company's staff, re-synthesized diacetylmorphine as a default in his attempt to produce codeine by a process of morphine acetylation. Instead of production of codeine, a less potent and less addictive drug, diacetylmorphine, twice as potent and addictive as morphine, was produced.

In 1898 and 1899, the Bayer Company registered and marketed diacetylmorphine under the brand name Heroin and acetylsalicylic acid, a reliever of minor aches and pains, as Aspirin, respectively. It was embarrassing for the company when their claim of a nonaddictive and analgesic diacetylmorphine was proven and exposed to still have the addictive property.

In 1914, the Harrison Narcotic Act was signed by President Woodrow Wilson. It declared narcotic use illegal except for medical purposes. The manufacture, importation, sale, and medical prescription of heroin and other opioid compounds were banned in 1924.

At present, heroin is placed under international control on Schedule I and IV of the Single Convention on Narcotic Drugs. It is illegal to manufacture, sell, or possess this substance without a license in some countries including the United Kingdom and United States of America. As diamorphine, this opioid can be provided under the management of a physician for long-term users in the United Kingdom.

Properties: The word heroin was derived from a German word "heroisch," meaning heroic. This was probably attributed to the moderate pain-reducing effect and alleviation of various breathing disorders like asthma, bronchitis, and tuberculosis. The opioids heroin, morphine, codeine, and other opium-based drugs cause opioid itch.

Opioids can cause CNS depression, resulting in cloudy mental function. Cloudiness and slowing thought processes are cognitive interference. Other side effects are constipation, nausea, vomiting, drowsiness, disorientation, delirium, and potential respiratory depression. This is the primary cause of death in heroin or morphine overdose. However, it is an excellent cough suppressant.

Heroin is usually injected, snorted, smoked, or orally administered. IV injection is the fastest route with most rapid onset of euphoria (7–8 s). The intramuscular route, called skin popping, is a relative slow route of onset of euphoria (5–8 min).

When heroin is snorted or sniffed, peak effects are usually felt within 10–15 min. Oral intake has the least rapidity of impact.

Action: Heroin is a strong painkiller as it activates natural opioid receptors in the brain and other sites reserved for endorphins. Endorphins are natural pain killers produced by the body in response to stress or pain. Thus, heroin blocks all pain transmissions from the spinal cord and brain stem. Activation of the opioid receptors in the limbic system (emotion processing site) produces euphoria resulting from the release of dopamine, the pleasure-producing agent. Regular users quickly develop tolerance, euphoria, moderate physical dependence, and severe psychological dependence.

The neurological effects of recreational use include analgesia, tolerance, and addiction (physical and intense, protracted psychological dependence). Major withdrawal symptoms peak between 24 and 28 h after the last dose of heroin and recede after about a week. Heroin withdrawal is not fatal if client is in healthy condition. However, the protracted psychological dependence could result in suicide.

Medical Complications: Scarred and collapsed veins, bacterial infections of the heart valves, vessels, abscesses, emboli, and other soft tissue infections are complications of chronic use of needles. Street heroin is cut by many soluble and insoluble additives that could result in the clogging of the blood vessels that lead to the lungs, liver, kidneys, or brain, resulting in infection or death of cells of vital organs.

Sharing of injection needles or fluids subjects the user to potential infections such as hepatitis B and C, HIV, and other blood-borne viruses.

Harm Reduction: A philosophy adopted by public health personnel to reduce harm associated with IV use of heroin, cocaine, and other psychoactive drugs for those still struggling with drug use. It is based on a pragmatic, nonjudgmental, and humane principle with the intent to promote hygienic injection practices and also encourage preferably other safer route of use.

The essence of the procedure is to minimize or completely arrest the transmission of blood-borne viral diseases such as hepatitis B, C, and HIV that otherwise complicate sharing of contaminated needles. It involves engaging individuals wherever they are in their unhealthy practices of drug use, moving them to increasing levels of improved self-care, health, and well-being.

The government-sponsored harm reduction program is an extensive financial and educational commitment that entails, first and foremost, confidentiality of the users. The government funds the needles and syringes exchange programs: delivery of the syringes and needles; education on the process of proper filtration before injection and safer injection practices and disposal of used needles.

Supplies may also include citric acid sachets/or vitamin C sachets, steri-cups, filters, sterile water, alcohol preinjection swabs, and tourniquets (to substitute use of shoe laces or belts).

An aspect of the harm reduction initiatives includes promoting a safer route of use such as smoking, nasal use, oral, or rectal insertion. This is preferred to the high risk of overdose, infections, and blood-borne viruses associated with injection of drugs into the body. As a precautionary measure, the use of small amounts of the drug at first, before further use, will assist in monitoring the strength and protect against danger and fatality due to overdose.

Users are also encouraged not to be alone when using, in case of accidental overdose. At the same time, the program discourages polydrug use.

In Canada, Europe, and Australia, harm reduction measures employed include safe injection sites for users where heroin and cocaine are injected under the supervision of medically trained personnel. This approach promotes safety and immediate intervention in case of complications in the process of use.

Prescription medicine addiction is currently a great concern. The abuse of prescribed medication is highly prevalent in most states and has reached epidemic proportions in Florida and California. The most common groups of medication abused are narcotics prescribed as pain medicine. These opiates are generally highly potent, with analgesic and addictive properties. They will reduce pain, alter mood, change behavior, and may induce sleep or stupor. Narcotic derivatives are widely prescribed in clinical management of acute or chronic pain, preoperative pain management, and postoperative pain reduction.

Some patients become addicted within a short duration of use, even under medically supervised prescription. Abusers may make multiple appointments with more than one doctor to obtain a variety of narcotic medications primarily to feed an addiction. Some users will ingest multiple drug mixtures such as a combination of alcohol and narcotics which are often lethal, due to the synergistic effects of these depressants. The result: respiratory center depression and sudden death.

Common narcotic pain medicines include methadone, morphine, oxycontin, Darvocet, Vicodin, and Lortab. There are narcotic cough medicines that contain codeine, hydrocodone, or dihydrocodeine.

Oxycontin is referred to as OC, OX, OXY, Oxycontin, and Kicker. The drug was introduced in 1996. This form of opiate was first prescribed as a painkiller for the treatment of moderate-to-severe pain, but illicit use of the drug escalated until it became an abusive drug of choice. The tablets can be chewed, crushed, and snorted like cocaine. The drug can be crushed, dissolved in water, and injected like heroin. The compound contains oxycodone, a derivative of opium, and is produced in a time-release tablet.

Serious side effects include respiratory depression which can be particularly dangerous for the elderly. Oxycontin has resulted in extremely high demands: pharmacies have been robbed and prescriptions are forged to obtain the opiate. It is estimated that oxycontin addiction (by people aged 12 or older) increased from 1.9 million in 2002 to 3.1 million in 2004.

Case Study: Maria, from Surgery to Addiction (From Author's Clinical Diary)

Part of my internship included ER work in a military hospital. I was on call one Friday night when at about 2:15 a.m., a 17-year-old female named Maria, a victim of a road traffic accident (RTA) arrived in the ER. She was conscious, well oriented in time and space, with vital signs slightly elevated and possibly shock induced. Her presenting complaints were cuts and bleeding from her scalp, headache, and generalized body aches.

Observation: Her scalp had a jagged cut, a third-degree deep tissue injury included a fleshy scalp flap contaminated with debris which flipped and rolled toward the forehead to reveal the skull bone. She was placed on IV fluid and provided an analgesic and a blood transfusion.

Diagnostic imaging revealed no hematoma (blood accumulation in the brain) and no skull fracture. The patient was relatively calm and cooperative. She was engaging and had brilliant recollection and great articulation in describing the events leading up to her injury. Pre-op and surgery went well. After the nursing staff shaved her head and she was stabilized, I had removed an extensive amount of debris and performed layer-to-layer suturing with absorbable catgut under analgesia and local anesthesia. Drainage tubes were inserted for blood and infection removal. Maria's initial stay in intensive care was uneventful. She was doing well on the third day in the surgical ward. The scalp wound was healing with a slight but serous discharge being managed through drainage. A sample was sent to the lab for M/C/S (microscopy culture and sensitivity) and came back as negative for infection. Her narcotic (morphine) dose was gradually stepped down. The drainage was removed. By the seventh day, the narcotic medication had been reduced to minimal dosages. She was stable and her wounds were healing. She was discharged and instructed to return for a consultation in two weeks. She was prescribed Vicodin p.r.n (to use as needed) for pain, and as part of a process of weaning her off the narcotic.

She showed up for her following appointment. Her request for more Vicodin medication raised concern that she might be abusing the narcotic. I referred her to the drug addiction counseling department for an assessment and spent time explaining the addictive nature of the drug. This was my last contact with her as I was on rotation to another department. About 9 months later, I received a call from the Psychiatric Department. It was sad news. I was informed that Maria had been admitted for drug-induced psychosis. I paid her a couple of visits. She was still the charismatic and intelligent lady I had known as a patient. She was excited to see me. Her scalp wound healed well and hair had grown back. She seemed to accept the reality of her situation and appeared committed to recovery from the illness. Her prognosis was good.

2.9 Drug-Screening Procedures

There are professionally designed and approved tests that serve as a clinical compass monitoring a client's functional compromise as related to the degree of abuse of alcohol and/or other psychoactive substances. The testing is often in form of questionnaires, interview process, and/or drug-detection examination. Below is a brief discussion of a few of these procedures.

Self-Administered Psychological Testing

Michigan Alcohol Screening Test (MAST)

A 22-question test, 1 point is allocated to each "Yes" answer, except questions 1 and 4, where 1 is allocated to each "No" answer.

0–2, no apparent problem,
3–5, early to middle problem drinker,
6 or more, problem drinker.

Drug Abuse Screening Test (DAST)

A 20-question test, 1 point allocated to each "Yes" answer.

0, no drug abuse reported,
1–5, low level,
6–10, moderate level,
11–15, substantial level,
16–20, severe level.

Alcohol Use Disorder Identification Test (AUDIT)

A 10-question test which is most commonly used in medical testing. A score of 8 or above is an identification of an alcohol problem.

Problem drinking is also detected by means of a questionnaire captioned *CAGE*. This most widely applied screening test only requires a positive response to one or two questions to confirm a habit:

* Have you ever felt the need to Cut down on your drinking?
* Have you ever felt Annoyed by someone criticizing your drinking?
* Have you ever felt Guilty about your drinking?
* Have you ever felt the need for an Eye-opener: an early morning drink to ensure normal function for the day?

Replacing A with U, is a newer substitution of CUGE for CAGE. The U question: Have you ever driven a vehicle Under the influence of alcohol?

Addiction Severity Index

Addiction Severity Index (ASI) is an assessment tool widely used in the evaluation of substance abuse treatment. This tool serves as a guidance instrument in treatment planning. This instrument is an interview process that assesses history, frequency, and consequences of alcohol and drug use.

Other commonly associated indicators of drug use: medical status, employment status, alcohol use, drug use, legal status, family relationships, social relationships, and psychological functioning are established with questionnaires administered by clinicians, researchers, or technicians. The higher a subject scores on the ASI, the greater the indication of a need for treatment. McLellan et al. (2004) concluded that ASI is a valid assessment tool.

Radioimmunoassay of Hair

This is a process employed in detecting abused drug of choice. This is based on a simple scientific fact: drugs, which are ingested, circulate in a person's bloodstream which nourishes the developing hair follicle. Trace amounts of the drug is impregnated on the core of the hair shaft in amounts roughly proportional to those consumed. These traces are retained in the hair as it grows out from the head at a rate of

Table 2.5 Other Substances that may Show Up in Patient's Drug Test as "False Positives"

Tested Drug	Substances in the Body that may Show a "False Positive" Reaction
Marijuana	Over-the-counter allergy preparations, sleep aids, and antinausea medications that contain Promethazine: Phenergan, Promethegan, Riboflavin (Vitamin B2), Edecrin, Dronabinol. Over-the-counter NSAIDS: Ibuprofen; Advil, Nuprin, Motrin, Mediprim, Excedrin IB caplets, Genpril, Naproxin, Midol, Aleve, Ketoprofen. Prescription NSAIDS: Clinoril, Dolobid, Feldene, Indocil, Anaprox, Tolectin, Ifenoprofen, etc.
Amphetamines	Over-the-counter cold and allergy remedies that contain ephedrine, pseudoephedrine, phenylephrine, or desoxyephedrine: Nyquil, Sinex, Sudafed, Dimetapp, Actifed, Neosynephrine, etc.
Cocaine	Amoxicillin, tonic water.
Opioids	Tylenol with codeine, poppy seeds, Emprin, Capital with codeine, Rifampicin, Percocet, Percodan, Vicodin, Wygesic, Margesic, etc.
Barbiturates	Donnatol, Fiorinol, antiasthmatic preparations that contain Phenobarbitol, Dilatin; Some sleeping pills, etc.
Benzodiazepines	Most prescription sleeping drugs and antianxiety medications.
LSD	Migraine medications: Egotamine, Ergostat, Caergot, Imitrex. Antinausea medications that contain Promethazine: Phenergan, Promethegan.

Table 2.6 Drug/Substance Detection Time

Drug/Substance	Detection Period	Drug/Substance	Detection Period
Cannabinoids (THC, Marijuana)	5–60 days	Benzodiazepines	7–10 days
Barbiturates (long acting)	3–4 weeks	Codeine	5–7 days
Cocaine	1–4 days	Barbiturates (short acting)	2 days
Amphetamines	2–5 days	Clenbuterol	4–6 days
LSD-ACID	7–10 days	Ketamine (special K)	5–7 days
Peptide hormones	Undetectable	Opiates	5–7 days
Nicotine (Cigarettes)	4–10 days	Methamphetamines	5–7 days
Euphorics (ecstasy, Shrooms)	5–7 days	Steroids (parenterally)	1–3 months
Steroids (anabolic oral)	14–28 days	Phencyclidine (PCP)	2–4 days
Phenobarbital	10–20 days	Propoxyphene	6 h to 2 days
Cannabinoids (THC, Marijuana) USE: one time	5–8 days		

approximately one-half inch per month. This could reflect a person's drug usage history of months and years past, as indicated on the hair, depending on the hair length.

The uniqueness of this proven drug testing procedure is the fact that it does not only detect if drugs of abuse have been used, but also it provides information in the quantity of drugs ingested by an individual and the historic pattern of drug use. Standard tests currently provide a 90-day history of drug use.

The radioimmunoassay hair testing process was originated in 1977 by Annette Baumgartner and Dr. Werner Baumgartner. The 10-year funding of research of this procedure is attributed to the Veteran's Administration, the National Institute of Justice, the American Society for Industrial Security, and the US Navy. The thousands of individuals subjected to this procedure have established the validity of drugs deposited in the hair which can be measured by ultrasensitive gas chromatography/mass spectrometry and radioimmunoassay procedures.

There are substances or chemicals that may show up in a patient's drug test as "False Positive" for a specific psychoactive drug. This is often caused by patient's intake of related medication, food substances, or metabolic products that bear similar chemistry to the particular psychoactive drug and is given in Table 2.5.

Drug/Substance Detection Time

Drug presence and detection in the body is a function of the unique chemistry of the particular drug/substance and biochemical interaction in the individual. This complex dynamic is reflected in the drug/substance rate of metabolism, storage, and elimination from the body. Table 2.6 shows an average detection period of ingested drug/substance.

3 Management of Addiction

The fundamental principle of disease management is treating the cause. Recurrence can be minimized or prevented by adopting a healthy lifestyle and by changing or ameliorating toxic environments that may interfere with creating healthy habits. Psychotherapy and pharmacotherapy are often combined in treating alcoholism and drug addiction, especially when intrinsic factors are diagnosed. Pharmacotherapy may serve as a replacement therapy, especially in "gene-deficit" clients. Pharmacotherapy should be a hand-in-glove therapeutic method with psychotherapy in cases that involve dual diagnoses (co-occurring disorders). Genetic variance may demand an individualized genetic profile and appropriate replacement therapy.

The causes of addiction are mostly interactive and complex, so treatments are simultaneously and carefully delivered to mitigate causative factors, with a purpose of ensuring ultimate recovery and long-term wellness. A therapist's dexterity is absolutely essential in this process because a variety of skills and tools need to be employed: active and reflective listening, respect, empathy, sympathy, a nonjudgmental stance, and positive attitude toward the clients. These tools can enhance feelings of security, trust, and effective relaxation in clients and create a bond between clients and therapists/counselors that promote optimal productivity in the course of clinical management. A professional competence is crucial in deferential diagnosis, that is, identifying dual diagnosis (co-occurring disorders) and other etiological factors that need immediate and appropriate referral.

1. Admitting there is a problem is the first step on the road to recovery, accompanied by consistency and a long-term commitment to treatment, sobriety, and recovery.
2. Withdrawal symptoms result from physical or physiological adaptations to an addictive drug when an abrupt cessation of intake takes place.
3. Pharmacotherapy/detoxification serves as a prelude to more extended treatment. Detox medications may include Methadone, Bupremorphine, Naltrexone, and Ibogaine.
4. Exploration of management entails evaluation or assessment as in Sections 3.1–3.3 and in Section 5.13 in order to arrive at the specific diagnosis and ultimate treatment.

3.1 Evaluation/Assessment

Evaluation of a client is essential for arriving at an accurate diagnosis and formulating an appropriate treatment plan. This can facilitate a client's cooperation and input toward relapse prevention in achieving successful treatment.

Practical Skills and Clinical Management of Alcoholism and Drug Addiction.
DOI: http://dx.doi.org/10.1016/B978-0-12-398518-7.00003-1

A formal assessment process usually includes a set of questionnaires employed by a therapist to gather broad and highly relevant information. These questions focus on demographics, precipitating circumstances, family and medical history, education, employment, legal issues, psychosexual history, general development, drug and alcohol history, and cultural, religious, or spiritual background.

These relevant pieces of information can serve as vital guidelines for arriving at an axial diagnosis and appropriate treatment plan. Clients' feelings of security, trust, effective relaxation, honesty, and steadfast behavior are paramount in the assessment process. Bonding established during assessment may vary according to a therapist's relative ingenuity in demonstrating active and reflective listening, respect, empathy, sympathy, a nonjudgmental stance, and positive attitude. An in-depth knowledge can also be essential in "connecting the dots" of clinical signs and symptoms derived from an examination of client information.

The "stages of change" model was developed by James Procheska and Carlos Diclemente. Clients present for assessment at any stage intercepted by relapse. These stages range from absolute denial to maintenance and possible relapse.

1. *Precontemplation*: A stage of complete denial. Client is not considering change in the problem behavior.
2. *Contemplation*: A stage of client's ambivalence toward change. He or she considers making a change, but not on a consistent level.
3. *Preparation*: The client has reached a decision to change and attempts to begin the process.
4. *Action*: A serious focus on change. The process of change has commenced. He or she begins to change specific problem behavior.
5. *Maintenance*: A consistent commitment to sustaining the new, healthy behavior.
6. *Relapse*: Retrogression to problem behavior.

Clients who relapse in the course of treatment have a better prognosis for sobriety if they return immediately to treatment. Patients seem to learn best from mistakes

A Case Study: Familial Depression (From Author's Clinical Diary)

John, a 23-year-old, African American male, showed up for a post-relapse assessment. His medical history indicated he was stabilized on methadone. John has been regularly attending one-on-one therapy, group counseling, and Narcotics Anonymous (NA). He claimed to have been sober for over eight months before his present relapse. He indicated in response to questioning that he was not aware of any personal or family history of psychiatric illness or depression.

However, a detailed history reveals otherwise. He claimed his older sister slept most of the day and night; she had pulled out virtually every strand of hair from her head, becoming bald within a course of a year.

In John's words, "Breathing is a job for me." Happy feelings had not crossed his mind for a long time. John revealed how he had struggled with sobriety until the relapse. He was referred to a psychiatrist as a dual diagnosis: depression and heroin addiction. An antidepressant was added to his medication regimen. He was consistent in his attendance of counseling sessions, support groups, and adopting a healthy lifestyle.

The prognosis was good. John has been sober for 2 years and is still doing well.

with the guidance and support of a therapist/counselor. A client who hits rock bottom may often yearn for treatment. This readiness for treatment can be facilitated by self-awareness, assessment, and other directed question-intervention strategies.

3.2   Motivational Interviewing

Sometimes clients attend an assessment in a state of ambivalence. They may show up at the clinic because they fear devastating consequences due to pressure from a significant other, family, friend, or employer who firmly demands that the client make a choice or forces the client to face the reality of their own mortality. Yet, addicted patients are more often than not in denial, ignoring problem behaviors and remaining indecisive about making a change.

Motivational interviewing (MI) is congruent to the concepts of motivational enhancement therapy, a person-centered therapy that is nonauthoritarian in approach and focuses on the client's internal motivation as the vehicle of effecting positive change.

A change from an ambivalent mindset to a state of self-diagnosis, self-awareness, and self-acceptance regarding their illness is a necessary step allowing clients to make the decision for treatment or progression in the course of treatment. This is the goal the therapist hopes to achieve during MI. The procedure could be anxiety provoking. However, the essence of MI is establishing a therapy-focused relationship and providing a safe environment for the client.

MI is a conceptual framework detailed in the work of two clinical psychologists, Professor William R. Miller, PhD, and Professor Stephen Rollick, PhD. This technique is a client-centered, semi-directive method that stimulates intrinsic motivation to effect change. In order to resolve the client's ambivalence toward changing addictive behavior, a doctor or therapist employs exploration therapy, creating an atmosphere conducive to change with the therapist's empathy and encouragement. This is most often facilitated by "rolling" with resistance and providing opportunities for introspection and self-awareness.

MI is rooted in psychological analysis of behavioral ambivalence and/or denial and is designed specifically for the treatment of addiction. This can also be an engaging tool for nurturing medical adherence and encouraging medication compliance to relieve the symptoms of probation behaviors that are associated with smoking, anxiety disorder, diabetes, cholesterol, diet and exercise, prenatal behavior, and infectious disease as well.

The most important motivational element of MI is empathy expressed by the therapist to establish a rapport with the client. This is done by communicating an understanding of the client's perspective and individual situation. Other psychological skills that are employed in order to help establish an atmosphere of trust, care, and credibility in therapist–client interactions are active and reflective listening, respect, nonjudgmental stance, and a positive attitude.

The strategy of rolling with resistance is often employed by a therapist in accepting a client's reluctance to change as a possible natural ground and avoiding any argumentative situation which might otherwise present itself.

Discrepancy developed by a therapist may introduce an awareness of the contradiction between a client's values and their addictive behavior. Exploration of this situation can provide insight that might effect a progression from contemplation to the stage of preparation (determination)—a decision to change.

Self-confidence and self-efficacy exhibited by the client must be embraced by the therapist even in the case of reluctance to change. The therapist's consistency and encouragement toward success can be accomplished through insight-oriented, open-ended questioning that is empathetic, respectful, and preserves the client's confidence while respecting his or her rights.

Thus, MI can be defined as an established dynamic of verbal interaction between therapist and client, which graduates from resistance to talk about change. Change comes from the will and motivation of the patient. A successful result evokes commitment from the client.

Here is an example of MI, a "classroom" study that gives insight into MI application. This demonstrates how these elements and concepts serve as guiding principles for an interview.

MI Transcript

Therapist: Hi, I'm Samuel.
Client: Hi Samuel, I'm Susan.
Therapist: How are you, Susan?
Client: I'm good.
Therapist: Welcome to the clinic. What actually brings you here today?
Client: My husband said I need to come in and talk to you about my drinking.
Therapist: Does anyone else know that you are here today?
Client: No, just my husband.
Therapist: What would happen if you do not keep this appointment?
Client: I think my husband would take my son and leave.
Therapist: Is he the father?
Client: Yeah. My son is the only child we have.
Therapist: Your husband would take the child and leave you ... if you did not keep this appointment? Is that exactly ... what he said to you? **(Bottom line: His plan if you don't show up at the clinic)** What did he say? **(A third-party question—the third party in this dialogue is her husband. His response will be crucial.)**
Client: He didn't say it, but I think that he probably would.
Therapist: Do you care if he does?
Client: Yeah, I do care a lot. I love my son. It would be very painful for me and I'll be so sad.
Therapist: Tell me about the relationship between you and ... your husband. How are you getting along? **(Decoding an insight into the family dynamics)**
Client: I think it's good. I love him a lot and I think he really loves me and our son, and that I cherish very much. He is a great man and a wonderful husband.
Therapist: How long have you two been married?
Client: Ten years.

Therapist: How old is your son?

Client: He is nine.

Therapist: How is your relationship with your son? **(Decoding—insight into relationship with their son)**

Client: It's good. We have fun together. He's a nice boy. His happiness is my joy. We're inseparable!

Therapist: I heard you say that your husband is the one who … referred you to this place for this assessment. **(Heat—the ultimatum her husband imposed is the cause of her discomfort)**

Client: Yes.

Therapist: And you think that if you did not come here today, … he is going to take the child and walk away from you? **(A reflective summary of the bottom line)**

Client: Yeah. And I don't want that to happen.

Therapist: I observe from your expression that you are not happy … about this. **(Response to feelings)** Tell me, what … exactly happened that made him tell you to come … here for an assessment?

Client: Two nights ago, our son had his first recital at his school. It was a piano recital. It started at 6:30 p.m., and we planned to meet there after work. My husband gets off work earlier than I do, so he agreed to pick up our son at the babysitter's. I was supposed to leave the office and meet them at the school. Unfortunately, I went out with some friends from work to have a drink.

Therapist: What was your plan?

Client: It was a co-worker's birthday. My intention was to just have one drink; then, I was going to leave for our son's school to attend his recital.

Therapist: I hear you saying that on this particular day your son's recital was scheduled at his school, your husband left work earlier and picked up your son at the babysitter's. You were supposed to join them at the recital. You went out with some co-workers to celebrate a birthday intending only to have one drink. **(Summary to promote active and reflective listening)**

Client: Yes, I intended to only have one drink.

Therapist: And what happened?

Client: So we were having drinks, some people walked in … they had to stay later; someone bought a round of drinks … old friends dropped in … And then I don't know; it just got to be a party, then one drink led to another and then pretty soon I forgot that I had plans. Then I didn't leave the bar for several hours.

Therapist: Did you make it to the school for your son's recital?

Client: No, I—I didn't make it to the school. I didn't see my son's recital.

Therapist: Well, what did your husband say? **(Third-party question)**

Client: He was really upset. He called me several times. I did not respond because my phone was turned off. He thought that something had happened to me. After our son's recital he took him home and started calling around for me. I returned home around 10:30 p.m. He was very angry at me.

Therapist: So, I heard you say that some friends came over to where you were having the birthday party; some others also stopped by, one drink led to another and you forgot to go to your son's school to see his recital. Is that what happened? **(Summary)**

Client: Yes.

Therapist: How did you feel about that?

Client: I felt embarrassed. My son was really upset with me.

Therapist: It sounds you didn't like the situation. It's obvious from your tone of voice that you wish it never happened. **(Linkage of feelings to "loss of control" experience)**

Client: Yes. I intended to have one drink.

Therapist: You were having a party.

Client: It was a party.

Therapist: A party in your own words. What does it mean to you? **(Decoding—exploring the meaning)**

Client: Well, we started laughing and having a good time, then someone ordered a round of drinks. They were putting it on the business expense so it wasn't a big deal. Then the band started playing and we were having a great time until I remembered that I had not called my family and not gone to my son's recital. It was a huge mess.

Therapist: What you are saying is—if I understand you right—that the forgetfulness is related to drinking beyond your control?

Client: Yeah, everyone was drinking.

Therapist: Okay, let me ask you this: do you normally have this forgetfulness when you are not engaged in out of control drinking?

Client: No. Really, I'm very organized. I know exactly where I need to be and I'm always punctual. I hate tardiness.

Therapist: So it was one drink too many that created the situation?

Client: I think so.

Therapist: When you got home, what did your husband say?

Client: He was not pleased with me.

Therapist: Did he know or think that you have been drinking?

Client: I was very drunk; he told me I smelled of alcohol.

Therapist: So he was aware that you have been drinking.

Client: Yes, he knew.

Therapist: How did you feel?

Client: I really felt bad.

Therapist: Do we both agree that out of control drinking was the cause of your forgetfulness? **(Linkage of feelings to "loss of control" experience)**

Client: Yes, that's true.

Therapist: And we also agree that you are here because you don't want to lose your family. **(Bottom line)**

Client: I don't. I'll do anything to avoid that.

Therapist: Okay, so that's why you are here today, right?
Client: Yeah.
Therapist: Aside from the current situation, has there been a prior occasion that your drinking has caused a conflict between you and your husband? **(Historical perspective—any history of her drinking resulting in similar situations, i.e., loss of control)**
Client: Yes. About 2–3 months ago, I don't remember exactly, it was a Saturday and I had a bunch of errands to run. I ran into a friend of mine; we took a pottery class together last year; so she called me that morning and wanted to have lunch. I told her it had to be a late lunch because I had a lot of things to do. I went to meet her at 2 o'clock. I was just going to have a salad and a glass of wine with her. We started laughing and sharing and "yada, yada, yada," one thing led to another and I got tipsy that afternoon. I had, I don't know, I thought it was about three glasses but she said it was five.
Therapist: Can you describe "one thing led to another" in your words? **(Decoding)**
Client: Well, we started drinking and then we had another glass of wine. I started getting a little light-headed and we had another glass of wine, and we had another glass of wine. That's all it means.
               By the time I got home, it was late. My husband was angry with me.
Therapist: At about what time did you get home?
Client: We had lunch from 2 p.m. until about 7:00 p.m. I didn't get home until around 8:00 p.m.
Therapist: And what time do you usually get home?
Client: Normally, on Saturday I am home all day.
Therapist: Was he expecting you at home earlier? What did he say? **(Third party)**
Client: Well, we had planned to go out that evening. We were expected to meet some of his friends from work for dinner at 6:00 p.m.
Therapist: Let me have a full understanding of the sequence of events that led to the situation. I'm hearing you say that you were out shopping and you met a friend of yours.
Client: Yeah, we had arranged to have a late lunch.
Therapist: So you had a late lunch with drinks. **(Summary)**
Client: We had a late lunch with wine and we kept drinking one after another.
Therapist: Was that your plan for the day?
Client: I had plans to meet with her for about 1 h, have lunch with one glass of wine, and that was it; I had other things to do …. Then she picked up the tab and proved to me that each of us had five glasses of wine. So I did drink more than I thought I would.
Therapist: In other words, you had a nice lunch with your friend and more drinks than what you intended. You made it home at 8:00 p.m. You missed the scheduled outing with your husband. Did I relate the sequence of events well? **(Summary of the first loss of control, evoking discrepancy)**
Client: That's correct. He had to go alone.

Therapist:	How do you think he felt about it?
Client:	Terrible.
Therapist:	Tell me, after this first situation, what did he say to you? Did you make any promise? **(Third party)**
Client:	You know, he was really upset and since then he has not been happy with me taking night classes. He wasn't happy and he doesn't trust me anymore. Well, I told him I wouldn't see her again. That it wouldn't happen again; that I would stop drinking. I said whatever was going to appease him and it worked!
Therapist:	Did you make a promise to him?
Client:	I did.
Therapist:	So you made a promise to him that it would never happen again. **(CCM—capture the client mind question)** What I hear you saying is that you went out to lunch with your friend for what was supposed to be 1 h and you were having a good time. You were enjoying being together and eventually you had some drinks: you had about five glasses of wine .... **(Summary)**
Client:	Five glasses of wine.
Therapist:	It appeared you were inebriated, according to your narrative, and apparently, forgot about your appointment with your husband ....
Client:	Yes.
Therapist:	And at that time, on that occasion, you made a promise that it would never happen again. **(Summary of #1 LOC + CCM—#1 LOC = 1st loss of control)**
Client:	Yes.
Therapist:	This last time, you went out with your co-workers to a bar; some co-worker was celebrating a birthday. You went to have one drink, but the one drink led to another and you forgot to show up at your son's piano recital. **(Summary of #2 LOC + CCM—#2 LOC = 2nd loss of control)**
Client:	Yes.
Therapist:	I believe from your account and reaction that these incidences were out of your control and unpleasant to you. **(Responding to the feeling)**
Client:	I'm embarrassed and I feel bad about it.
Therapist:	In view of these events, are you apprehensive of the impact on the relationship with your husband?
Client:	Yes.
Therapist:	Are you concerned that your drinking is threatening your marriage? **(Anchor point)**
Client:	To tell you the truth, sometimes I'm scared and confused ... but most times I'm not worried about my drinking. But my husband is more concerned.
Therapist:	Are you worried about losing your husband and family? **(Value)**
Client:	Yes .... It crosses my mind, sometimes.

Therapist: Are you concerned that your drinking may be causing a conflict and threatening the continuation of your marriage? (**PAP—presenting anchor points**)

Client: Drinking makes me happy ... Well, maybe a mistake here and there crosses the line, which is my bad ... But my husband is just a worry wart.

Therapist: It seems to me you are not much concerned about your drinking. (**Rolling with resistance**)

Client: Well, I think he's just blowing it all out of proportion. He doesn't drink a lot. He occasionally has a glass of wine.

Therapist: Okay, let's assume that's a possibility. But from his perspective, you failed to show up at your son's recital as planned because you were out drinking with friends and forgot all about it. Prior to this latest incidence, you went out to lunch with a girlfriend but didn't get home until 8 p.m. You missed the scheduled outing with your husband to a 6:00 p.m. dinner with his friends from work. On both occasions, your intention was to have one drink. But that didn't happen. You admitted you lost control of your drinking. From his point of view, you've got a problem. But from yours, you seem ambivalent. (**Value**)

Client: Yeah. He's uncomfortable with my drinking habit; this is not a serious issue for me; but I still love him anyway and I want my family.

Therapist: If you have any word to use, what would you call someone who abuses alcohol? (**Eliciting the word**)

Client: What? I don't understand.

Therapist: Your word to describe someone who has a problem with alcohol. (**Eliciting the word**)

Client: An alcoholic?

Therapist: How would you know if someone has crossed the line into alcoholism? (**Eliciting the definition**)

Client: I suppose if they need it; if they kept using, because they need it; if they couldn't have fun without it.

Therapist: Have you ever come across anybody in your family setting or friends that have crossed that line into alcoholism or drug addiction? (**Building a bridge to mutual definition**)

Client: I have a lot of brothers, one is an alcoholic. And my grandfather died from complications of alcoholism.

Therapist: So there is a family history. Would you put it that way?

Client: Yeah.

Therapist: Tell me, how do you describe your brother's actions that have convinced you that he's an alcoholic?

Client: Because he drinks all of the time. You know, he never goes out without drinking. He's just an unreliable person. When he starts drinking, he gets unreliable.

Therapist: Does he make promises he doesn't keep? (**Eliciting the definition**)

Client: Yeah, yeah.

Therapist: In your words, someone who's an alcoholic is someone who drinks all the time and does not keep promises?

Client: Right. But actually, he doesn't drink all of the time, but most times he does. And he gets really stupid, he can't remember what time it is or keep time ....

Therapist: Do you think because of this behavior, he pays some consequence for his actions?

Client: Well, yeah, because no one really relies on him.

Therapist: How would you place yourself with your experience? I would like to know whether alcohol affects you keeping your promises. Does it disturb your keeping promises? **(Eliciting a self-diagnosis)**

Client: Yeah.

Therapist: Okay, let's talk about your "two times." On the two occasions, you've told me about how your drinking had an effect on your ability to keep promises? Do any consequences come with it?

Client: Yeah. The last two times that I went out, I didn't keep my promises. And it had a consequence. My husband is not pleased with me. He doesn't trust me.

Therapist: Is that because you are unreliable?

Client: Yes.

Therapist: You also gave me a picture of your brother's situation. That when he drinks sometimes, he is irresponsible; doesn't keep his appointments, and he's unreliable.

Client: Yes.

Therapist: Now look at the situation here; two instances; you were not able to meet your husband for an appointment because you were drinking with your friend on that Saturday shopping trip and also another, you could not make it to the school for your son's piano recital because you were with your co-workers drinking.

Client: That's true.

Therapist: Based on your description of your brother, do you think you have a problem with alcohol? I want you to reflect on our conversation about your issue with alcohol use. **(Eliciting self-diagnosis)**

Client: Well, I hadn't thought of it that way, but you know, it sounds like my brother.

Therapist: Can you relate your situation to your brother's? **(Responding to the feeling)**

Client: Yeah. It is scary to admit. But it is really an eye-opener for me. **(The Ah-hah moment)**

Therapist: Let's look at it this way. Because we have this agreement about your drinking, I'm going to put alcoholism/addiction on a scale of 1 to 10. One is someone who drinks frequently, but is still functional and has no memory problems or experience of negative consequences. Ten is someone who drinks more than what he/she wants to drink, past his/her intention frequently and has lost everything, sometimes to the

	point of death. On this scale, where would you put your situation? **(Continuum of self-diagnosis)**
Client:	Maybe at six. **(Self-diagnosis)**
Therapist:	And how would you place your brother?
Client:	He's probably at eight or nine.
Therapist:	You put yourself at six, right?
Client:	Yeah, at six.
Therapist:	At this point, you seem to have an insight of the effect of your alcohol use. Committing to treatment would improve your health status and save your relationship with your husband.
Client:	I am disappointed, I'm very upset with myself that it took me this long to come to this realization.
Therapist:	**(Reframing: conversion of client's emotional turmoil into good sign or a positive shift)** Coming into a place of self-acceptance of your problem drinking can be an uncomfortable feeling for you but it is a sign of progress and a new beginning. Many people are initially scared when they have an insight into their addiction, but this awareness and acceptance is a gradual but significant first step on the road to recovery through commitment to treatment. We are going to be there for you; in support and assistance with your treatment. It's going to be a collaboration of efforts on both sides. We are going to work on a plan that is feasible for you; you'll have to tell me how you are going to accomplish this, with my assistance. Your commitment is very essential to the achievement of your treatment.
Client:	I understand a lot more now. I will check into treatment. I am committed to getting better. **(A shift from contemplation to the preparation (determination) stage)**

When the client finally arrives at a place of self-realization and self-acceptance of his/her pathology—addiction—self-determination to a long-term commitment to treatment is often his/her progressive pathway. Along with a strong family support and professional assistance, the client's prognosis or chance of wellness can be promising.

3.3 Classification Format of Pathologies

Holistic management is ensured by broad and relevant diagnostic criteria, as reflected in the classification format of pathologies as follows:

The DSM-IV-TR (Diagnostic and Statistical Manual of Mental Disorders 4th Text Revision) five-level diagnostic axial classification model is concise and explicit, representing the clinical pathologies indicated for effective treatment plan.

Axis I: This is the primary diagnosis; the presenting complaints often identified in multiple ways:

    Alcohol dependence
    Opiate dependence

Panic disorder

Post-traumatic stress disorder.

Axis II: This is for personality disorders or mental retardation:

Antisocial personality disorder

Narcissistic personality disorder

Histrionic personality disorder

Dependent personality disorder

Borderline personality disorder.

Axis III: Includes medical or physical disorders presented:

Peptic ulcer

Hypothyroidism

Constipation.

Axis IV: This is reserved for stress factors aggravating the current psychiatric disorder and mitigating treatment outcomes:

Financial difficulties

Social issues

Legal problems

Lack of a support system.

Axis V: Global assessment functioning (abbreviated as GAF). This axis is assessed on a 100-point tool rating. This describes a comprehensive mental health level or performance in usual daily activities based on psychological, social, and occupational functioning as to degree of wellness. A score of 81 and above is deemed to be within the normal bounds of functional mental coordination.

3.4 Treatment

These "Axes" of pathologies present the treatment focus and widely accepted referrals essential in holistic management of a client. A *treatment plan* is an individual outline for remediation developed after an evaluation. This plan is regularly monitored for effectiveness. The engagement between the client and therapist helps to identify a client's challenges and strengths and a plan is proposed that is feasible to the client. The plan is put in place and constantly reviewed leading to the ultimate goal of treatment and rehabilitation. For the agreement to be binding as well as to eliminate legal complications, both parties must endorse the plan and keep a copy for reference.

A *problem* statement: These are problems specifically identified by clients as being traceable to individual challenges. These could be familial or genetic, environmental or extrinsic, or some synergistic combination. A well-conducted assessment may reveal other significant information like denial or delusions and associated etiologies (depression, psychiatric disorders, and physical or physiopathology) that may be causative factors as well. Not all information is problem-oriented, as some orientations come from a place of strength in the client and might be employed in planning treatment.

A *goal* statement: The client's willing admission of their problem and commitment to achieving and maintaining sobriety and recovery through the treatment plan is the ultimate goal. However, there have been circumstances where clients declared their intention to retain their addiction. This may happen in chronic cases of use, chronic or terminal illness, or severe psychiatric disorders in dual diagnosis (co-occurring disorders). Referrals to appropriate medical departments as well as harm-reduction programs (see Chapter 2) have been helpful.

Measurable objectives are strategic steps to reach the goal. Strategic steps are treatment modalities administered and measured as the progress that is monitored through assessment. This measurable objective approach is an indication of a clear pathway to achieving a goal.

4 Theories of Treatment

Effective treatment partly involves the application of theories of human behavior. These theories are fundamentals of human behavioral psychology that are part and parcel of an eclectic practice. In summary, these theories form the basis of psychotherapy.

Other strategic tools are support groups (aftercare programs), special focus groups, and pharmacotherapy (drug therapy) as follows.

4.1 Psychotherapy

Psychotherapy is an individual (one-on-one) or group "talk" therapy during which evidence-based practice concepts are applied to modify a client's behavior and effect change. Presently, this remediation is the most prevalent method for treating alcohol and drug addiction through therapy. This long-term process produces the most useful outcome when combined with other supportive therapies.

A good deal of significant research-based evidence characterizes the conceptual frameworks for psychotherapy. Although, there are no hard and fast rules when applying these concepts, and combinations of various treatment modalities can be very effective depending on the compatibility of theoretical constructs when applied in individual or group counseling.

Adlerian Theory

Individual psychology was developed by Alfred Adler, an ophthalmologist and general practitioner in Vienna. In 1902, Adler was invited by Sigmund Freud to an informal discussion group that became the genesis of the psychoanalytic movement, or the "Wednesday Society," because the meetings took place every Wednesday. Adler became the president of the Vienna Psychoanalytic Society 8 years later. In 1911, he formally disengaged from Freudian psychoanalysis and biological determinism.

In 1912, he founded the Society of Individual Psychology. Adlerian theory is a growth model that emphasizes the positive attitude of human nature and control of one's own destiny, rather than just being a victim. He suggested that early in life, we create a unique lifestyle that stays relatively constant throughout our lives.

Adler's theory says we are motivated by goal-setting and purposeful behavior to reach for perfection and superiority. Each of us may encounter challenges or become involved in a variety of social interests which change our journey. The intent of Adlerian therapy is to challenge and encourage a client's goals and aspirations. To achieve this, a therapist will gather as much family history as is available and learn

Practical Skills and Clinical Management of Alcoholism and Drug Addiction.
DOI: http://dx.doi.org/10.1016/B978-0-12-398518-7.00004-3

about the client's past performance. Then the client and therapist set a goal which is not too low or too high and can be supported and achieved. This support can be demonstrated in a healthy, respectful relationship based on mutual trust. The therapist may assign homework to stimulate client enthusiasm toward achieving a goal. Over time, Adlerian therapy encourages psychoactive chemical-dependent patients to discontinue use and become contributing members of society. This therapeutic modality has also been used to improve parenting and marital skills, as well as to encourage many resolutions of life challenges.

Behavior Therapy

A concept of learning to overcome specific behavioral problems, this therapy holds that behaviors are learned and we are a product of our environment. The therapy is based on learning new behaviors by eliminating unwanted behavior through self-management, assertion, behavioral rehearsal, cognitive restructuring, relaxation, and other behavior modification methods. The therapist and client both actively participate in learning more desirable behavior which is effective in managing depression, phobias, sexual disorders, children's behavioral disorders, and stuttering.

This widely applied clinical behavior modification theory is based on *operant* conditioning (B.F. Skinner). Skinner based this conditioning theory on the concept that learning is a function of change in overt behavior with reinforcement as the key element in stimulus–response theory. Thus, reinforcement strengthens change and may include a broad range of cognitive phenomenon.

Classical "Pavlovian" conditioning forms an association between two stimuli. Stimuli that animals react to without training are called primary or unconditioned stimuli (US): food, pain, and electric shock. These are instinctive or "hardwired" stimuli. Stimuli that animals react to only after learning about them are secondary or conditioned stimuli (CS). This is the fundamental principle for training animals. The capacity for association of unrelated stimuli with timely application is called classical conditioning. A clinical example is salivation and drooling in response to the appearance of food (US). Initially, when a bell ring (CS) is applied prior to the food presentation, the drooling was insignificant. After several repetitions of the stimuli, it was discovered that the bell ring (CS) produced as much salivation and drooling as when the food (US) appeared.

Social Cognitive Theory

Social cognitive theory is a concept of learning through modeling. Albert Bandura (1974) described *"modeling"* as a learned behavior that comes naturally by observing what happens to others within the context of social interactions, experiences, and media influences.

Bandura demonstrated the concept of modeling or social cognitive theory by the following experiment:

Bobo Doll Behavior: A Study of Aggression —In this behavioral study, a group of children were exposed to a video, featuring violent and aggressive actions. On completion of the exposure, they were placed in a room with a Bobo doll to observe their behavior with the doll. The children subjected the doll to a violent and aggressive treatment, unlike other children who did not watch the violent video. The inference from the experiment: The children reenacted the model of violence they learned from the video, which may explain how people reenact behaviors learned from media influence. A classic example is the use of celebrities' endorsements to market products to certain demographics. The effectiveness is elevated when a particular gender, age, and ethnicity is employed in communicating the message to a particular target group.

Another instance worth citing is in the education arena. Teachers play a role as a model in the acquisition of learning both in academics and moral etiquette that promotes self-efficacy in students.

There is a high correlation between the social cognitive theory and outcome expectancies. The environment that the individual grows up in is a significant factor that heavily influences outcome expectancies. For example, children raised in alcoholic homes are more likely to become alcoholics themselves, just as those who come from an abusive home tend to become abusers.

Rational-Emotive-Behavioral Therapy

Albert Ellis developed a counseling method which addresses the role of cognition as an important element of human behavior. Rational-emotive-behavioral therapy (REBT) deals with a client's cognitive and moral state. This method indicates we are born with rational thinking, but may fall victim to irrationality. The rational-emotive-behavioral therapist believes that a client's problems are rooted in childhood and belief systems formulated during childhood.

The therapist establishes relationship with a client and focuses on helping to change attitudes, beliefs, and negative self-statements that drive and maintain problematic behavior. An overriding principle of REBT is that events do not disturb people, but the view (belief, attitude) that clients may take of events is what leads to dysfunction.

The ABC Model of REBT

A—Activating events: negative life events that someone confronts.
B—Beliefs: how a client thinks or feels about activating events.
C—Consequence: anxiety and frustration may result from consequences which propel dysfunctional beliefs.

REBT contends the consequences are less worthy of discussion than the beliefs fueling problematic behavior.

Cognitive-Behavioral Therapy

Aaron T. Beck, MD, was influenced by Albert Ellis' rational-emotive-behavioral counseling. Aaron Beck's CBT model further enhances cognitive and behavioral skills building. Beck's model includes how we think (cognition), feel (emotion), and act (behavior). All these functions interacting together determine our feelings and behavior. Beck claims personality is developed and shaped by internal cognitive schemas: drivers that influence personal views, beliefs, internal values, and life assumptions. These schemas guide interaction and processing of stimuli during times of stress.

CBT is an inquisitive probe into the clinical integration of cognition, emotion, and behavior. Other therapy models attempt to answer "why" questions, while CBT answers "what keeps them doing it?" and "how do they change?" These "what" questions address reinforcing mechanisms that maintain patterns of thought, affect, and behavior. "How" questions relate to skills building. This merging of behavior and cognitive therapy focuses on the "here and now" in alleviating symptoms.

Socratic dialogue (questioning session) during and after the facilitation of a small group by a therapist encourages participants to think independently, logically, and critically. This enhances self-confidence and encourages a search for the truth in response to specific questions. A client's dysfunctional thinking often comes from internal processing errors or systemic bias error. This defines cognitive bias: a pattern of deviation in judgment, leading to irrationality. Irrationality could be described as perceptual distortion, inaccurate judgment, or illogical interpretation of reality.

Examples of Systemic Bias Thinking (Dysfunctional Thinking)

Polarized thinking (black and white thinking)
Overgeneralization
Labeling and mislabeling
Magnification and minimization
Selective abstraction
Arbitrary interference (fortune-teller error)
Personalization
Mind reading.

Albert Ellis' design of "ABC" techniques for irrational beliefs sheds analytic light on cognitive therapy.

A—Activating event that lead to negative dysfunctional thinking.
B—Beliefs: negative thoughts that occurred as a result of an event.
C—Consequence: negative feelings and dysfunctional behavior precipitated: anger, anxiety, sorrow, etc.

Therapeutic questioning assists clients in uncovering dysfunctional thinking errors. This process includes questions and conversational dialogues calculated to gently bring insights to the surface. Thinking errors create "automatic" thoughts; dialogue provides an opportunity for a counselor to question the validity of these automatic thoughts. This process is often where cognitive shifts can occur so that clients assume control of their thinking. These shifts allow the client to recognize and avoid negative schemas and misrepresentations. This clinical model of cognitive restructuring allows a client to separate fact from fiction. It promotes self-enhancement, self-empowerment that ensures positive behavior modification. This is a model that is fundamentally relevant to contemporary psychotherapy.

Triple-Column Technique of CBT

A proven practice for improvising internal self-critical dialogue. David D. Burns, MD, designed a method for developing an effective self-evaluation system. The method can be applied to document self-critical thoughts.

During this evaluation, a client can identify distortions and learn why thoughts may be distorted. Clients can "talk back" to distorted thoughts—responding to them in order to develop a realistic self-evaluation system. This is clinically managed by a process called "reframing" and involves identification of irrational beliefs. Therapists work with a client in challenging negative thoughts from the client's experience and reframing these thoughts: an approach that boosts self-esteem, self-confidence, and promotes assertiveness. This serves as a recipe for healthy mental, emotional, and rational thought processing. Successful reframing encourages a client to develop rational beliefs and healthy coping mechanisms.

Burn's third column, "Rational Response," is a product of reframing (Table 4.1). The intent appears to strengthen clients' coping strategies.

"Reframing" Concept Based on Work by Burns

- Draw three columns as in Table 4.1 (Burns, 1999).
- List critical thoughts (self-criticism) in first column.
- Identify cognitive distortions—Learn why these thoughts are distorted (second column).
- Rational Response—Talk back to your distorted thoughts. Develop rational thought from the process (third column).

Table 4.1 Representation of Triple-Column Technique

First Column	Second Column	Third Column
Automatic Thoughts (AT)	**Cognitive Distortion Identified (CDI)**	**Rational Response (Self-Defense) to AT**
"I always make wrong choices."	Overgeneralization	"Not true! My choices are right most of the time!"
"Everyone thinks I'm a criminal."	Labeling	
	Mind Reading Polarized Thinking Overgeneralization "All-or-Nothing" Thinking	"I'm not a criminal. And the erroneous thought or judgment is absurd and unacceptable!"
"I'll be ashamed of myself if I show up."	Labeling, Fortune-teller Error	"Nothing to be ashamed of! I'm a person with dignity and pride. My presence will be welcomed."

Scripts are of author's original design. First column—List of automatic thoughts (from thinking errors, self-criticism); second column—Identification of cognitive distortions; and third column—Identification of rational thoughts.

Cognitive Distortions: Listed below are 10 distorted thinking patterns that are basis for identifying client's thinking errors or distortions:

- All-or-nothing thinking
- Overgeneralization
- Disqualifying the positive
- Jump to conclusion (mind reading, fortune-teller error)
- Mental filter
- Emotional reasoning
- Magnification or minimization
- Labeling and mislabeling
- Personalization
- Should statement.

Ultimate Goal of "Reframing" Session

- Defeat negative self-talk,
- Improve internal self-critical dialogue,
- A positive shift from a critic to a coach of inner dialogue dynamics.

The "Reframing" process promotes cognitive restructuring that fosters rational thinking. This elevated state of self-esteem, self-confidence, assertiveness, and rationality is a progressive step in the course of treatment of alcohol and drug addiction.

CBT is an effective counseling method that advances a break in the addiction cycle and addresses core issues. As discussed earlier, other concepts such as the Triple-Column Technique and Albert Ellis' ABC technique are insightful elements of CBT. They enhance the mechanism of cognitive restructuring that translates into a positive behavior modification.

CBT is largely effective when delivered short term. This may include visits with a psychologist or psychotherapist that demands for active participation. Exercises in independence, self-reliance, and personal responsibility indicate successful therapy. Long-term psychotherapy, without clear goals, may support dependence on a psychologist or prescribed medication. This can enhance feelings of permanent disability, promote irrational thoughts, and may lead to further illness, which is a waste of time and resources for the client seeking a stable recovery.

CBT is a treatment of choice for a number of mental health issues: PTSD, clinical depression, hopelessness, suicidal ideation, anxiety, bulimia nervosa, and neurological conditions such as myalgic encephalomyelitis (chronic fatigue syndrome).

Dialectical Behavior Therapy

Dialectical behavior therapy (DBT) was developed by Marsha M. Linehan, a psychology researcher at University of Washington, for treating patients with borderline personality disorder (BPD). DBT combines CBT, an emotion-regulation technique, and reality testing with concepts of distress tolerance, acceptance, and mindful awareness, largely a product of Buddhist meditative practice.

A person with BPD is "emotionally vulnerable," someone whose ANS is extremely sensitive to stress that presents with excessive reaction to low dose of it. Also, return time to baseline after removal of stress is prolonged compared to normalcy. Biological diathesis is conceptualized to be responsible. An emotionally vulnerable child, further subjected to emotional trauma of an "invalidating environment" presented by significant others in his/her life further complicate the lack of skills for emotion modulation. In view of these overwhelming vulnerabilities, a state of "emotional dysregulation" is precipitated which produces the typical symptoms of BPD.

BPD patients are mostly female and have proven to be very difficult in therapy because of failure to respond to therapeutic efforts. The considerable demands on therapists' emotional resources are daunting, especially in a critical situation of prominent suicidal and parasuicidal behaviors.

DBT recognizes the multiple dialectical dilemmas that are fundamental behavioral pathologies of BPD. Therapy is structured clearly in stages and at each stage a definite hierarchy of targets is defined. The patient is helped to understand her problem behaviors and how to deal with them more effectively. DBT provides a technique of treatment of this difficult group which offers hope as well as preserves the morale of the therapist. Also, it is therapeutic in the management of behavior associated with sequence of mood disorders inclusive of self-injury. Effectiveness with treatment of sexual abuse and chemical dependency is evident.

Gestalt Therapy (Meaningful Whole)

Developed by Frederick "Fritz" Perls II, Gestalt therapy integrates body and mind factors by stressing awareness. Integration of feelings, behavior, and thinking is the primary goal. Clients must become aware of what they are doing, how they are doing it, and how they can change. They must learn to accept and value themselves.

This phenomenological perspective allows clients to depart from usual ways of thinking so that they can tell the difference between what is actually being perceived and felt in the current situation and what is residue from the past. Gestalt therapy addresses "subjective" feelings in the present and "objective" observations as real and important data. This is preferable to evasiveness and substituting interpretation to derive meanings.

Gestalt phenomenological exploration may enhance awareness or insight about feelings, thoughts, and learning personal responsibility. This can help the patient regain control and change unhealthy behavior. The "empty chair" technique is one of the various ways in which Gestalt therapy can be applied. In this exercise, the patient role-plays both characters in a situation. The patient alternates between two chairs that are three feet apart and face one another. This allows a patient to experience being both characters in examining feelings or emotional conflicts and attitudes associated with each character. The therapist may say, "Imagine your father or someone you're having an issue with is occupying the empty chair." This objective and subjective data, combined in confrontational techniques, encourages ownership of behavior versus thinking others are responsible. This process allows patients to become more understanding and learn new behaviors in the supportive therapeutic environment. This is both a cognitive and effective behavioral change, increasing levels of awareness. The clients learn to handle unpleasant emotions without fleeing or resorting to drugs or alcohol. These alternative responses can be applied to other surprises the patient may encounter. Gestalt techniques have been successfully employed in treating psychotic disorders, severe character disorders, and a wide range of psychosomatic disorders including migraine, ulcerative colitis, and spastic neck and back.

Existential Theory

This addresses a patient's view of the world. There are three components essential to human relationships and survival.

> *Unwelt*—environmental and biological—internal drives, instincts, and needs,
> *Mitwelt*—personal community that focuses on interpersonal relationships,
> *Eigenwelt*—self-awareness and self-relatedness.

Existential theory promotes insight and prompt discovery of the root causes of anxiety. The therapy reflects on the essence of these components and focuses on how freedom of choice can reshape a life. Emphasis is placed on the present and future where the therapist encourages freedom of expression and stresses personal responsibility rather than surrendering to "destiny," and each client is encouraged to find an individual path. The focus is on "how" questions about one's behavior and puts less emphasis on "why."

Motivational Enhancement Therapy

A nonauthoritarian method of counseling based on a patient's internal motivation as a driving force for changing problem behavior. MET is grounded in the clinical approach known as MI (Miller & Rollnick, 1991). MET is similar to person-centered therapy in the belief that change comes directly from the will and motivation of the patient. MET attempts to de-emphasize labels and focus on the patient's personal choices. This method is nonauthoritarian because it sees resistance to treatment as an opportunity for reflection and deliberation. These fundamental principles of motivational psychology are often more useful than argumentation.

The role of the counselor is supportive allowing the patient to guide the change. The pathway to change will be navigated through the "stages of change" model developed by James Procheska and Carlos Diclemente (see Section 3.1).

Person-Centered Therapy

Created by Carl Rogers, this is known as nondirective counseling, client-centered therapy, or Rogerian psychotherapy. The nondirective nature of this method provides evidence that the client, rather than the counselor, can help direct the treatment process by evoking self-change. The counselor–client dynamics invests trust in the client to move in a positive direction, provided that the counselor demonstrates appropriate skills: active listening, genuineness, and paraphrasing. A practitioner must be nonjudgmental and avoid giving advice. This supportive role will help clients feel accepted and allow them to understand their feelings. This humanistic therapy acknowledges and focuses on conscious perceptions rather than some therapist's presuppositions and ideas regarding "unconscious" mindsets.

Person-centered therapy most often demands more responsibility from the client. An "actualizing tendency" in every living organism is the survival instinct: this internal dynamic leads people toward growth, development, and realization of their fullest potential. Person-centered therapy is a positive, directional form based on release and support.

Psychoanalytical Therapy

Founded by Sigmund Freud, this is the deterministic approach to counseling. Psychoanalysts believe that childhood events and unconscious feelings, thoughts, and motivations play a large role in mental illness and maladaptive behaviors. They offer an empathetic and nonjudgmental environment where the patient can feel safe in revealing feelings or actions that have led to stress or tension. This environment facilitates treatment. Often times, simply sharing these burdens with another person can have a beneficial influence. The "unconscious mind" is believed to be the storage of painful memories and the intent of the therapy is to bring the repressed material to a conscious level for understanding, deliberation, and resolution through a process called analysis of resistance. Psychoanalytic therapy embraces trust, empathy, and nonjudgment to provide a healthy avenue for a client to better articulate painful emotions. This is meant to promote tolerance of these emotions and more proactive responses in future situations.

There are three components of the unconscious state in psychoanalytic therapy:

Id—the source of unconscious, aggressive, and sexual urges,
Superego—the source of moral urges,
Ego—the mediator between the id and the superego.

In the course of therapy, the nature of unconscious mental processes and conflicts are revealed and resolved so that personality restructuring can be accomplished. This is intended to reinstate the ego as director of the mind. This insight-oriented therapy is of great benefit to clients who suffer from recurrent relapse and deep-seated personality disturbances. Self-medication of internal pain or wrongly dealing with specific negative emotional states is often the cause of psychoactive chemical abuse.

Psychoanalysis assists in early identification of dysfunctional dynamics in a client's family and early childhood. Knowledge and self-awareness is intended to reduce unconscious cravings for alcohol and drug use and identify a constant internal rage. This conflict is brought to consciousness and effectively addressed. The use of negative defense mechanisms is decreased to further lower or discourage substance abuse.

Reality/Choice Control Therapy

In reality/choice control therapy, developed by Dr. William Glasser, there are five basic needs we are always pursuing.

Power—includes achievement, feeling worthwhile, and winning.
Love and Belonging—includes the feeling of being a part of groups, family, and loved ones' lives.
Freedom—includes independence, autonomy, and one's "own space."
Fun—includes pleasure and enjoyment.
Survival—includes nourishment, shelter, and sex.

In any unsatisfactory situation that is distressing or troubling, we need to examine whether or not we are effectively meeting basic psychological needs for power, belonging, freedom, fun, and survival. Our drives, as social beings, are defined as our wants more than our needs. Here are some reality check questions:

What do you want?
What are you doing to get what you want?
Is it working?

The counselor sets up a feasible plan for the client to achieve goals and desires. Healthy therapy empowers clients to take control of their lives. For example, maybe a client cannot make a spouse talk; but can talk to the spouse. This is a positive way of asserting control; however, any attempt to impose control on others often leads to pain and frustration.

In reality therapy, the past is seen as the source of wants and reflects our behavior. We have good and bad in our lives. The focus is to learn what we need to learn about the past and quickly shift to empower our needs and wants to better deal with the present and future. This is a therapy of hope and conviction which suggests that even though we are products of the past, we are not victims. As such, doing is the heart of reality therapy. Changing what we do is the key to changing how we feel and getting what we want. Our choice of what we do may be the best decision we ever make—choice theory.

As presented above, it is evident that theories of human behavior are the foundation of psychotherapy. In treatment, psychotherapy is often combined with other strategic tools to ensure ultimate prognosis in drug addiction management.

4.2   Support Groups (Aftercare Programs)

A 12-step support group adheres to the 12 steps of Alcoholic Anonymous (AA) which is grounded in spiritual orientation that encourages participants to admit being powerless over their addiction and to commit their recovery to a higher power. AA was founded in 1935 by Bill Wilson, a stockbroker, and Bob Smith, a physician, two alcoholics who helped each other to sobriety through fellowshipping, and then carried their message to others. A 12-step support group becomes the most prevalent support group in the clients' communities. This mutual support can promote abstinence from alcohol and drugs and positive interpersonal relationships. These programs are just a few of the groups that use the 12-step formula:

AA (Alcoholics Anonymous)
NA (Narcotics Anonymous)
Cocaine Anonymous
Co-Dependents Anonymous
Al-Anon
Alateen
Overeaters Anonymous
Debtors Anonymous.

12-Step Program

The original 12-step program as published by AA is as follows:

1. We admitted we were *powerless* over alcohol—that our lives had become unmanageable.
2. Came to believe that a power greater than ourselves could restore us to sanity.
3. Made a decision to turn our will and our lives over to the care of the *God* we understood.
4. Made a searching and fearless moral inventory of ourselves.
5. Admitted to God, to ourselves, and to another human being the exact nature of our wrongs.
6. Were entirely ready to have God remove all these defects of *character*.
7. Humbly asked a higher power to remove our shortcomings.
8. Made a list of all persons we had harmed, and became willing to make *amends* to them all.
9. Made direct amends to such people wherever possible, except when to do so would injure them or others.
10. Continued to take personal inventory and when we were wrong promptly admitted it.
11. Sought, through *prayer* and *meditation*, to improve our conscious contact with God, praying only for knowledge of God's will for us and the power to carry that out.
12. Having had a spiritual awakening as the result of these Steps, we tried to carry this message to alcoholics, and to practice these principles in all our affairs.

It should be mentioned that in some cases, where other AA groups have adopted the 12 steps as guiding principles, the steps have been altered to emphasize principles important to particular fellowships. Sometimes this involves removing gender bias or specific religious language.

Alternatives to 12-Step Groups

There are many support-model groups that are actively opposed to the religious or spiritual tone found in the 12-step groups and employ more psychological and less sectarian approaches.

Smart Recovery
Rational Recovery
LifeRing Secular Recovery
Secular Organization for Sobriety (SOS)
The Lenair Techniques
Women for Sobriety (WFS).

Smart Recovery

Self-management and recovery training is a nonprofit organization that offers globally self-empowering, science-based mutual help groups promoting abstinence from alcohol, drugs, gambling abuse, and addictions. This program assists individuals in gaining independence from addictive behaviors based on contemporary scientific knowledge. The program equips clients with skills that enhance and maintain self-motivation, coping mechanisms, problem-solving skills, and lifestyle balance.

Rational Recovery

Rational Recovery (RR) was founded in 1986 by Jack Trimpey, a California-licensed clinical social worker. This "for profit" organization is offered through the Internet, books, videos, and lectures.

RR does not regard alcoholism as a disease, but rather as voluntary behavior. RR is rooted in the principles of CBT and REBT. The RR program is based on the premise that an addict is capable of permanent, planned abstinence. At the same time, RR therapists recognize that an addict, paradoxically, wishes to continue using. This is because addicts believe in the power of a substance to quell anxiety; an anxiety which is partially substance induced and enhanced by the substance. This ambivalence is the RR's definition of addiction and the treatment is self-empowerment with positive cognitive thinking to promote positive decisions.

Trimpey calls the "addictive voice" powerful and related to brain control of our outcome survival functions. When the voice of the "beast" is not satiated, the addict experiences anxiety, depression, restlessness, irritability, and anhedonia (the inability to feel pleasure). The RR method is to commit to planned permanent abstinence from the undesirable substance or behavior and a mental adaptation or discipline to the commitment.

The RR program is based on recognizing and defeating what the program refers to as the "addictive voice," internal thoughts that support self-intoxication and addictive impulses.

LifeRing Secular Recovery

LifeRing Secular Recovery or LSR is a secular, nonprofit organization that provides peer-run addiction recovery groups for anyone who is committed to recovering from addictions or who are in relationships with alcoholics or drug addicts. LifeRing was incorporated in 1999 after separating from SOS and operates internationally.

LifeRing encourages the incorporation of ideas or processes of abstinence from individuals or groups to ensure and maintain sobriety. The organization provides resources to teach members to use relapse as a learning experience and does not chastise the member involved. The three principles of LifeRing's philosophy are sobriety, secularity, and self-help. Sobriety is a commitment to abstinence from alcohol and addictive drugs. Secularity is the exclusion of spirituality, that is, meetings are not opened with prayers and do not mention or recognize a supreme being. Self-help encourages individuals to develop their own program of recovery.

The groups are led by peers and not by professionals. Members are allowed to give each other feedback when anyone requests it. Members do not have sponsors, but are encouraged to help each other.

Secular Organizations for Sobriety

The SOS movement began with an article in the summer of 1985 by James Christopher, the son of an alcoholic himself. He wrote "Sobriety without Superstition" as an account of his path to sobriety. He claims that his path led him through 17 years of fearfulness, guilty alcoholism, and intermittent fearful and guilty sobriety with Alcoholics Anonymous. He was convinced that there were other alcoholics who wanted to achieve and maintain sobriety through personal responsibility and self-reliance rather than by turning one's life over to a higher power. He strongly believes in the science of etiology of addiction as our physiology not psychopathology. SOS groups are now in every state and in other countries.

In November 1987, the California courts recognized SOS as an alternative to AA in sentencing offenders to mandatory participation programs. The Veterans Administration has ruled out mandatory participation in programs of religious nature.

Women for Sobriety

WFS is an organization and a self-help program for women alcoholics. WFS has been providing services for women alcoholics since July of 1975. The group was founded by Jean Kirkpatrick, PhD. This organization strives to address female issues in a male-dominated world and provides an alternative to the AA philosophy of admission to powerlessness and submission to a "male" God. WFS emphasizes the potential for change women can make rather than focusing on powerlessness. WFS works cooperatively with AA and recognizes that some women benefit from working with both organizations.

The Lenair Technique

Since 1985, Ms. Rhonda Lenair, an energy healer and the founder of the Lenair Technique, has helped many clients who were suffering with a wide range of addictive, emotional, and stress-related problems. Clients from around the globe come to see her based on documented success and the words of those who respect her work. Her hands-on technique is an integration of electromagnetic and bioelectric modalities to effectively create change. Ms. Lenair's energy system is adapted to the bioelectrical systems of each client. Her resources target an explicit problem such as addiction.

Ms. Lenair does not subscribe to any particular school of thought or philosophy concerning health; the world at large is her resource when she is in her energetic state and she brings that expertise to her healing practice.

4.3 Special Focus Programs

There are numerous special focus programs that are directed toward and supportive of the management of addiction: faith-based treatment, holistic treatment, relapse prevention, dual diagnosis (co-occurring disorder) programs, self-help programs, Methadone clinics, depression treatment, and Alternative Incarceration Programs (AIP), to name a few.

Some of these programs will be discussed under pharmacotherapy (Chapter 6), but the AIP will be our main focus in this section.

Alternative Incarceration Program

These are intensive prison programs offered by the Oregon Department of Correction (DOC) to selected inmates who are at risk of reoffending due to untreated addictions and criminal thinking. Eligibility for the program can be established when a prisoner is convicted of burglaries, identity theft, and drug manufacturing and distribution. Other potential clients include those charged with attempted rape in some instances and/or DUI accidents that maimed victims. Felony sex offenders and Measure 11 prisoners are disqualified from participating. A judge can exercise discretionary power to bar participation if there is a substantial and compelling reason based on the prisoner's record. AIP graduates are often released after serving 25–75% of their sentence.

There are presently three programs in operation. The Summit (Success Using Motivation, Morale, Intensity, and Treatment) Program began in 1994 at the Shutter Creek Correctional Institution in North Bend. The program is open to both men and women. Summit graduates approximately 225 inmates annually.

The 2003 Legislature approved AIPs including "Turning Point" for women and "New Directions" for men (Table 4.2). These provide cognitive-behavioral change programs that focus on addiction treatment.

Table 4.2 Oregon Department of Corrections Completion Rates by Program for All Inmates in A&D Programming Inmates Released in January 1, 2009, through December 31, 2009

Location	Program	Completion Type	A&D Number Completing	A&D Percent Completing
CCCF	Turning Point (Female)	Administrative	2	1.8
CCCF	Turning Point (Female)	**Failure**	16	14.2
CCCF	Turning Point (Female)	**Success**	95	84.1
CRCI	Turning Point (Male)	Administrative	6	5.2
CRCI	Turning Point (Male)	**Failure**	22	19.1
CRCI	Turning Point (Male)	**Success**	87	75.7
PRCF	New Directions	Administrative	7	1.9
PRCF	New Directions	**Failure**	58	15.7
PRCF	New Directions	**Success**	304	82.4
			597	

Source: Research and Evaluation Unit-Scorecard-ad_comp_by_program_2008.rtf
Administrative—a transitive shift of clients; CCCF, Coffee Creek Correctional Facility; CRCI, Columbia River Correctional Facility; and PRCF, Powder River Correctional Facility.
Bold text emphasis on the result of the program
The success rate, an attainment of sobriety, mental, and psychological stability by a client in the AIP program, is much higher than the failure rate as research result in Table 4.2 infers. This is an indication of the effectiveness of AIP. A study of recidivism rates of AIP graduates is essential. Lower or decreased rates of recidivism will indicate higher or increased rates of maintenance of sobriety or recovery. Maintenance of sobriety or recovery is the ultimate goal of addiction treatment.

Turning Point is offered at Coffee Creek Correctional Facility in Wilsonville, which serves about 100 women yearly. New Directions for men is an intensive residential treatment program at Powder River Correctional Facility in Baker City and provides skills training programs for about 350 men each year. The program sets its focus on developing personal accountability and responsibility through a structured daily routine that involves physical work, exercise, and behavioral skills development.

Group and individual addiction treatment tools include 12-step and other recovery activities where participants learn the skills necessary to change their behavior and increase their personal accountability and responsibility. Additional interventions prepare inmates for gainful employment and teach them how to develop and maintain pro-social relationships and family skills. Participants learn to identify and change criminal thinking errors and develop healthy decision-making skills and habits for successful community living.

The eligibility criteria include first an application from an inmate. The inmate must satisfy a minimum qualification which considers the legal status of their crime and sentencing along with risk factors that include alcohol and drug abuse. Active participation is required as inmates may lose their privilege at any time for rule infractions, lack of effort or motivation, poor progress, or lack of positive change. An inmate may request to be removed from the program at any time.

The author's clinical experience as an alcohol and drug addiction therapist/counselor with New Direction inmates was educational and inspiring. This out-patient therapy program is the last phase of the AIP program during which inmates are released into the community under the guidance and monitoring of parole officers and the Powder River Correctional Facility Management. They are mandated to attend counseling at a specified clinic as well as secure jobs within 30 days. Their living arrangement is the clients' responsibility. The goal of this phase is assessing active participation in developing skills offered by the out-patient program.

The program focuses on personal responsibility, accountability, achieving and maintaining sobriety, and recovery. The participants are exposed to basic survival needs: finding shelter and searching for employment. Besides the one-on-one or group counseling based upon the 12-step program and CBT, counselors often address stressors in the client's life including concerns pertaining to a job search, maintaining a job, and finding shelter.

The most commonly identified problems are personality defects which include low self-esteem, paranoia, delusions, and impaired judgment. These issues, often revealed through intake questionnaires, treatment, and relapse prevention plan, are frequent topics for individual or group counseling discussion. Regular and full participation in facilitated discussion sessions are beneficial to clients, promoting cognitive restructuring and consequent positive behavior modification, essential for clients' rehabilitation. Each client is offered this opportunity to make a positive change. Individual progress is reinforced with release from incarceration.

Some of the clients' employers are compassionate and take a personal interest in their employed clients, going as far as attending their client's therapy sessions and offering to take part in any way they can in order to ensure a successful treatment and reintroduction of the client into the community.

There are stresses: emotional and psychological impact at initial exposure of clients to the community. This rehabilitation process however takes its course and should be emphasized that it is necessary to allow adjustment to the society. The follow-up case study demonstrates some difficulty in rehabilitation that a client experiences in the community.

Case Study: Charles' Paranoia (From Author's Clinical Diary)

It was a group counseling session. At the beginning of the session, a check-in time is optional and gives clients an opportunity to share their situations. They may discuss the past, present, or any conflicts they're facing that need assistance with resolution. Clients may address these conflicts through interactive communication in the group counseling session. This allows clients to receive feedback if they choose.

On this occasion, everyone had participated and it was Charles' turn to share. Charles claimed that, two days prior, he was on a commercial bus when a police car turned their sirens on about three blocks behind the bus and was driving toward them. He experienced a sudden surge of his heart rate and irrational fear and anxiety that depicted a "flight reaction." He was seated at the back of the bus and found himself leaping from his seat and racing up to the front of the bus. He witnessed an uneasy reaction to his behavior in the bus driver who was slowing down in response to the emergency siren before Charles was able to get hold of himself and calm down.

Charles admitted to his paranoia and requested help in dealing with social adjustment in the community. This incident was one topic in this discussion that addressed self-esteem, paranoia, and delusions. Everyone participated and Charles welcomed the feedback.

Such sessions are usually busy. We resolve individual or group problems based on evidence-based practices and concepts that are applicable and pragmatic. The results are mixed. Some of the clients have graduated and gone on to live independent, well-adjusted and healthy lives in the community while others have suffered setbacks, lost their privileges, and returned to prison.

Frequent reasons for removal from the program include testing positive in urine tests for drug use, irregular attendance, bad behavior and poor attitude during sessions. AIP can give a chance of a lifetime to inmates in need of treatment for an addiction which is the cause of their criminal thinking. This intervention is intensively client-oriented and highly beneficial for inmates committed to positive life change.

5 The Impact and Treatment of Drug Addiction

Besides the self-destructive effect of drug addiction on an individual engaged in drug abuse, the dysfunctional behavior pattern has a negative impact on his/her environment. The effects of drug addiction on family dynamics, culture, women, older adults, mental illness, and LGBTQ (lesbians, gays, bisexuals, transgenders, and queers) are documented here. The placement criteria for treatment efficacy, support system, and psychotherapy are also subjects of discussion in this chapter.

5.1 Family and Drug Addiction

A healthy, functional family operates from a place of love, care, and concern for its members in such a delicate balance that consistency ensures behavior that fosters well-adjusted personalities in healthy interactions. Often unspoken roles and boundaries are culture and age defined as these nurture civil interpersonal relationships. The family constitutes an immediate social system that is vulnerable to dysfunction due to addictions.

When abuse or addiction strikes a family member, the impact ripples through the family structure. As a result, members of a family develop dysfunctional behavior patterns, assuming particular roles and functions in an attempt to cope. As made well known by Claudia Black, PhD, people often identify with some of these reactive personalities. Here are some of the more common roles.

The Enabler: This is a member of the family who is co-dependent on the addicted family member. An enabler expresses a maladaptive behavior that encourages or indulges the addiction. The enabler may be acting out of love, trying to help or protect the addict. Enabling behavior can be an indication of powerlessness, self-blaming, pity, acceptance of responsibility, or feelings of guilt. Manipulative behavior is a common tool in the relationship dynamic between enabler and addict.

The Hero: Another characterization of a family member. This family member defines his or her status with success, self-worth, and a high sense of responsibility and independence. This member also yearns for approval. Feelings of guilt, inadequacy, and hurt are common.

The Mascot: This is the clown of the family. The clown provides distraction with humor and hyperactivity in family interactions but suffers feeling of insecurity, fragility, and confusion.

The Lost Child: This person is withdrawn, aloof, quiet, distant, independent, and often overweight. This member may use food to medicate and deal with emotions of rage, fear, confusion, and hurt.

Practical Skills and Clinical Management of Alcoholism and Drug Addiction.
DOI: http://dx.doi.org/10.1016/B978-0-12-398518-7.00005-5

The Scapegoat: This is the family member who acts out and directs focus on the pathological family dynamic. This person is defiant, withdrawn, and tends to eventually become a psychoactive drug user. Feelings of anger, rejection, hurt, and fear are implosive internal reactions that may cause the scapegoat to depend too heavily on peers.

The Chemically Dependent Family Member: The ruin of a family is predicated upon drug addiction as reflected in the discussed family members' behavior reaction.

This personality expresses anger, aggression, compulsion, self-delusion of grandiosity, and a high degree of manipulation. This can result in feelings of shame, pain, and guilt. The family dysfunction is most devastating if either or both parents are struggling with the disease of addiction themselves. This disturbing situation is most often a recipe for child abuse, a lifelong nightmare for victims of this misfortune if treatment is not availed to them.

Pain, guilt, anger, rejection, confusion, rage, insecurity, inadequacy, and other negative emotional feelings are evidence of dysfunctional family dynamics associated with a psychoactive drug-dependent person. Treatment is indicated.

A holistic approach of treatment management addresses family history and impact. This entails assessment for the need for behavioral and medication evaluation referral. Improvement in coping mechanisms, problem-solving, self-esteem, and self-care skills; cognitive restructuring, stress management, and family education are crucial in the course of treatment of drug addiction in a family structure.

5.2 Culture and Addiction

Scientific evidence based on research studies makes it possible to conclude that addiction to alcohol and drugs cuts across gender, race, culture, religion or creed, and socioeconomic status. Addiction is largely due to genetic and environmental predisposition (see Chapter 1). Due to intrinsic (genetic) and extrinsic (environmental) etiologies, an estimated 22 million Americans aged 12 and up suffer from alcoholism and drug addiction (Substance Abuse and Mental Health Services Administration (SAMHSA)'s 2002 National Survey).

The American Psychiatrists Association reports that more men than women are included in an annual mortality rate of 100,000 deaths due to the compulsive use of illicit drugs and alcohol in the United States. The most vulnerable population is African Americans, constituting 12% of the US population. This disproportion is aptly addressed in this quote: "*In 1999, the African-Americans accounted for 23% of admissions to publicly-funded substance abuse treatment facilities. Consequently, there is a great need for more culturally sensitive and efficacious treatment targeted to the special needs of this minority population*" (Alice B. Britt, MSN, APRN, CS). The writer was not only concerned about the high number of African Americans admitted to treatment; her statement also suggested an effective treatment concept.

In 2006, SAMHSA data show 21.3% of admission of African Americans, 59.4% of White Americans, and 14% of Hispanic origin. The data still convey a relatively high rate of incidence among minority groups.

A fluctuating or increasing incidence of drug addiction and alcoholism in the minority population in particular and the entire population in general is of great concern.

No conventional group treatment approach has yet attained appreciable success. This is likely due to the lack of a culture-sensitive approach addressing specific issues that normally stymie progress toward recovery. A complementary culturally sensitive group forum for resolutions of emotional and psychological issues would promote the sobriety process and support recovery maintenance. (For further insight, see Section 5.10.)

5.3 Socio-Cultural Influence of Alcohol

In spite of the stark reality of the apparent doomed life of an alcoholic, "the skid-road bum" that is despised by the judgmental society, drinking alcohol is still generally regarded in the society as sophisticated and hospitality best served. This is not surprising in a society where the people are constantly bombarded by advertisements via electronics such as televisions, radio, smart phones, tablets, and commercial billboards, newspapers, magazines, and so forth. Advertisements primarily promote sales of products. Its psychological tools are sales of grand illusiveness and frequency of repetition. A classical product of advertising is alcohol in all forms and brands, ranging from beer and wine to the ultimate hard liquors such as scotch and so on. Commercials of alcohol have never stopped its amazement. Its nutritional value has never been the essence of sales nor the concern for inebriation that could result in fatality. The highlight of presentation is often about association with "the gentleman/woman of distinction" that depicts success, class, and taste of celebrities which are the dreams and wishes that lure society. Sometimes the satire of the commercial messages is so ludicrous that you most probably pretend to be deaf and blind at the same time or you are so addicted that nothing could stand in the way of you and alcohol use. The alcohol market is a very lucrative business and often most frequently patronized by abusers and addicts of alcoholic beverages.

Consumption of alcohol has been largely assumed to be a matter of social custom determined greatly by attitude prevalent in the culture. However, not every drinker of alcohol becomes an alcoholic. There must be other factors responsible for the etiology of the disease of alcoholism. Proven vulnerabilities are genetic (familial) predisposition, peer pressure, stress, PTSD, parental abuse/neglect, or interactions of these and other factors.

Whatever the reason for alcohol use, be it social or cultural, the quantity of regular consumption has a significant influence in determining our fate related to alcohol addiction.

Orthodox Jews use wine in rituals and at meals. But to be "drunk like Gentiles" is an abomination and undignified. In Paris, more drinking of hard liquor in social situations is tolerated, contrasting different cultural norms. Cultural understanding is crucial in treatment management and rehabilitation. This insight will prepare the client in a realistic and practical way with coping tools for maintenance of a healthy lifestyle in their own environment with its specific drinking practices and values.

The attitude of authorities and/or philanthropists in funding treatment programs should be a comprehensive understanding of the impact of alcoholism on the lives of members of the society as a public health problem and not through some prejudicial scope of ideology that could compromise coverage.

Another essential element in combating alcoholism in the community is a public prevention campaign. The approach must recognize the attitudes of societies especially in a permissive society that embraces use and misuse of alcohol as culturally acceptable practices reinforced by peer pressure. This liberalism seems to be best favored in the United States, a melting point of cultures of unimagined broad spectrum that varies from ultra-liberalism to neo-conservatism.

This explains the low percentage rate of recovery from alcoholism and drug addiction with present fit-it-all management that is largely applied. Also, it validates the essence of culture orientation of a client in treatment management as discussed in culture-centered management (see Section 5.10).

There is an urgent need for review of treatment management. Critical questions are: What are the factors of cognizance in a contemporary treatment management of alcoholism and drug addiction? These include culture (see Section 5.10); nutrition (see Section 6.6); spirituality (see Section 4.2); gender (see "Women for Sobriety" in Chapter 4); sexual minority (see Section 5.8); aging (see Section 5.5); mental illness (see Section 5.7); and other proven vulnerabilities, as mentioned earlier. The list with all its complexities goes on and research appears to be our ultimate pathway to success.

5.4 Women and Drug Addiction

Women most often progress differently in the course of treatment and as such require different treatment approaches, because 70% of drug-addicted women have a personal history that may obstruct treatment, progress, and recovery. Some of these reasons are as follows.

Women are more secretive with their habit primarily because they fear authorities intervening and taking their children. They also fear reproach and reprisal from spouses, boyfriends, family, and relations. Late presentation is compounded by serious physical and mental health issues such as poor nutrition, liver disease, low self-esteem, physical abuse, and depression.

If a woman is pregnant, addiction may cause congenital deformations of babies or pre-term labor and delivery. Multiple sex partners and use of contaminated needles in drug injections lead to serious medical and infectious diseases such as sexually transmitted diseases (STDs), hepatitis B and C, chlamydia, gonorrhea, HIV, and AIDS.

A higher prevalence of parental history of alcohol and drug abuse and history of drug using spouses or multiple male sexual partners are often cited as consequence of drug addiction. Women having issues with alcohol and drug use most often have low self-esteem, low self-confidence, and feel powerless.

Women benefit more from gender-specific treatment management which is reflected in core principles of gender-responsive treatment:

- Focusing on uniqueness of women's health and concerns,
- Promoting cultural suitability that is women specific,
- Encouraging developmental capabilities,
- Employing strength-based treatment paradigm for women.

Support groups such as Women for Sobriety Inc., a nonprofit organization, are dedicated to helping women overcome alcoholism and drug addiction. (For further reading, see "Women and Alcohol" in Chapter 2.)

5.5 Older Adults and Addiction

Scientific technologies have considerably improved the health care system. Health education contributes to heightened self-awareness, care, and healthy lifestyles by promoting regular exercise, intake of healthy, balanced nutritional diet and supplements, routine medical check-ups, and early detection and treatment of conditions. These integral factors are largely responsible for the increase in the population of older adults. At the same time, chronic diseases such as alcoholism and drug addiction strike the aging population, resulting in a higher rate of incidence of the disease.

It is important to note that the aging process affects how the body reacts to alcohol. The same amount of alcohol can have a greater impact as we grow older. If no adjustment is made to decrease alcohol consumption as we become older, the stressful effect on our body is more severe and we are more vulnerable to diseases.

The National Institute on Alcohol Abuse and Alcoholism, a section of the National Institute of Health, recommends no more than one drink a day at age 65 or older. This is risk-free level for this demographic. One drink is 12 ounces of beer or wine cooler; or one 5-ounce glass of wine or 1.5 ounces of 80-proof distilled spirit.

The signs and symptoms of older persons' alcoholism and addiction are poor self-care, neglect, withdrawal, isolation, confusion, and memory slips. These are often assumed to be part of normal process of aging or sometimes mistaken for aging-associated disease such as Alzheimer disease. It also increases the risk of work and household accidents such as falls and hip fractures. Incidence of car crashes is of concern among this demographic, knowing 10% of US drivers are over 65 years of age. Alcohol abuse or dependence does put people at risk of conflicts with spouses, family, friends, and coworkers.

Cardiovascular pathologies such as hypertension, heart and blood vessel damage are complications of alcoholism or alcohol abuse. This could result in cardiac failure or death. Chronic abuse can cause liver cirrhosis, cancers, immune system disorders, and brain damage.

Interactions between over-the-counter or prescribed medications and alcohol ingested are dangerous and sometimes fatal. An elderly alcoholic is vulnerable to this predicament because an average older adult is often on some medication for body rejuvenation or medical treatment.

The following are examples of risks of drug interactions with alcohol in the body system. Aspirin can cause bleeding in the stomach and intestine. If aspirin is taken while drinking alcohol, the risk of excessive bleeding is elevated. Cold and allergy (antihistamine) medications often cause drowsiness. When antihistamine medicines are taken while drinking alcohol, drowsiness and sleep can be aggravated.

Use of mass dosages of paracetamol (acetaminophen) with alcohol can raise the risk of liver damage. You should consult with your doctor or pharmacist of the risk of drinking alcohol with use of over-the-counter or prescribed medication.

In the United States, more than a million older adults are presently alcohol dependent and this number is estimated to rise to 23 million over the next 25 years. Little attention has been paid to alcohol-related problems in late life and very little research has been done to study the effects of alcohol on elderly adults. However, it is good to note that some organizations such as the American Society on Aging and the National Council on Aging have commenced an advocacy effort to address the issues.

In the last two decades, efforts have begun toward effective treatment and management of alcoholism in older adults. This approach involves identifying, assessing, treating, and rehabilitating elderly alcoholics.

The Center for Substance Abuse Treatment of the US Department of Health and Human Services (DHHS) published best practice guidelines in a federally sponsored treatment improvement protocol: Substance Abuse Among Older Adults—Treatment Improvement Protocol 26, DHHS Publication number (SMA)98-3179. The publication was based on specialized practices of treatment and care for older alcoholics by a few large organizations that are well-funded establishments with large resources that can afford and maintain multidisciplinary staff, providing services for wealthy clienteles.

The translation of this knowledge and skills as described in the protocol as best practices is of immense importance. The goal is to provide essential services in a variety of communities where financial and professional resources are highly compromised. These reasons or excuses of unavailability of funds and professional resources are difficulties encountered in the provision of treatment for older adult alcoholics on a large scale that benefits the masses.

A grassroots model of treatment proposed by Roland Atkinson, Professor of Psychiatry at Oregon Health Science University, and Frederic C. Blow, a senior research scientist at the University of Michigan, Department of Psychiatry, states: "...in which the realities of local resources and commitment determine the best strategy for delivering essential services to aging alcoholics in that particular community." This recommends screening for alcoholism by all providers in aging services, health care, and substance abuse, and calling for proper training and active role participation of these agencies in the community. When a case of alcoholism is confirmed, a professional referred to as the care manager is informed. He/She would establish a close working relationship with the client and could extend to the client's caregivers as needed.

The care manager draws the treatment plan for the drinking behavior recognizing associated physical, mental, and emotional ill health, and social problems for effective client-centered treatment. The care manager coordinates and executes the treatment plan in which the goal is sobriety and its maintenance. The concept seems pragmatic in terms of affordability, effectiveness, and broad outreach within the communities.

5.6 The Canadian Program

A fascinating and comprehensive program designed in Canada to provide services for older adults in treating alcoholism and drug addiction promotes a robust intervention that is beneficial to their communities.

The blurred boundaries of clinical presentations of alcoholism and drug addiction and normal indications of aging process limit services to alcoholic older adults. The recognition of this under-management welcomes Community Older Persons Alcohol (COPA), an outreach program designed to provide a comprehensive, efficacious, and client-centered service for the older adult population.

The COPA program was started in Toronto in 1983 by S.J. Saunders, a physician who recognized even at that time that alcohol and drug problems are not restricted to young people, and that when older people do have such problems they often manifest themselves in a variety of unexpected ways that make them difficult to detect and treat. This outreach program primarily cares for and caters to older adults in the community with a holistic approach that is client-centered wellness. This is completely different from traditional treatment principles.

The COPA program focuses on older people who are struggling with alcohol and drug problems and rather than assuming that addicts should come to the program, as they might in traditional treatment facilities, COPA reaches out to them. The treatment is delivered with empathy, respect, care, and a nonjudgmental attitude. Clients do not need to acknowledge substance problems in order to be eligible for assistance in attaining meaningful change. They receive counseling in their homes. COPA determines the needs of the elderly clients in consideration of their individual input. COPA accompanies clients to important appointments, advocates, and coordinates with other services and clients' families.

COPA is put on a referral list in case of crisis. This program serves to maintain independence for elderly clients in their homes and communities while raising awareness and making connections to other necessary community support services.

5.7 Mental Illness and Addiction

Addiction is common in people with mental health problems. According to reports published in the *Journal of the American Medical Association*, a source from the National Alliance on Mental Illness declares:

- *Roughly 50 percent of individuals with severe mental disorders are affected by substance abuse.*
- *37 percent of alcohol abusers and 53 percent of drug abusers also have at least one serious mental illness.*

- *Of all people diagnosed as mentally ill, 29 percent abuse either alcohol or drugs. Psychosis, a severe mental condition that causes one to lose touch with reality, possible causes are abuse of drugs and/or alcohol, manic depression, dementia, brain tumors, and strokes. Thus the variable causes of mental illness and/or alcohol, drug addictions are complex, interchangeable and a function of individual vulnerabilities. Addiction is a state of mental disorder. Is severity individualistic? Response is affirmative.*

A family history of mental disorders, such as unipolar and bipolar depression, anxiety, schizophrenia, borderline and other personality disorders, with alcohol or drug addiction, is evident of predisposition to comorbid disorder. Other causes of mental illness such as brain injury, congenital defect, or disease state are probable etiologies attributed to co-occurring disorder.

Andrew Chambers, MD, proposed "co-occurring disorder by a common cause" published in an American Psychological Association December 2, 2007, paper titled "Mental Illness and Drug Addiction May Co-occur due to Disturbance in the Brain's Seat of Anxiety and Fear." The experiment involved neonatal amygdala lesion (damage) of the experimental rats and the consequent co-occurring impact on social/fear-related behavior and cocaine sensitization in adult stage. It concluded that the integrity of the amygdala (the brain center that modulates fear, anxiety, and emotions in general) was the root cause of both impaired fear behavior and heightened drug response, suggesting an overall hypersensitivity to addictive process.

He further speculates, "*complex interactions among subtle genetic and environmental factors that change the way the amygdala functions or is connected to the rest of the brain during childhood and adolescence.*" As an example, Dr. Chambers indicates, "*early emotional trauma paired with certain genetic background may alter early development of neural networks intrinsic to the amygdala, resulting in a cascade of brain effects and functional changes that present in adulthood as a dual diagnosis disorder.*" Dual diagnosis or co-occurring disorder will continue to be a subject of contemporary research.

A current holistic management entails an integrated treatment regime of pharmacotherapy and psychotherapy administered by the combined efforts of educators, counselors, physicians, and scientific researchers that bring insight into the contemporary treatment skills. Strong supportive family and/or peer group system, support groups such as AA, NA, Al-Anon, and so on are indispensable.

5.8 Sexual Minorities (LGBTQ) and Addiction

The present wave of homophobia and discrimination against the LGBTQ population makes addiction treatment twice as difficult. The diversity and the high sensitivity level demands recognition, respect, and accommodation for special needs in the course of counseling and treatments. Understanding the struggle with being LGBTQ is critical to effective treatment of psychoactive drug addiction.

The National Association of Lesbian and Gay Addiction Professionals (NALGAP), founded in 1979, is dedicated to the prevention and treatment of alcoholism, substance abuse, and other addictions in the LGBTQ population. NALGAP provides information, training, networking, and advocacy about addiction and related problems and support for those engaged in the health profession, individuals in recovery, and others concerned about these populations. This organization provides a reliable and informative source for treating alcoholism and drug addiction in the community.

5.9 Addiction and Diseases ("Addicted" Brain, HIV/AIDS, Hepatitis)

Drug addiction is a chronic, relapsing brain disease that causes compulsive drug seeking in spite of the harmful consequences suffered by the addicted individual and those in his/her environment. What precedes addiction is often abuse of the psychoactive substance. In previous chapters, we discussed the causes of abuse/addiction:

1. Intrinsic (genetic) factors that are related to causation of addiction as depicted by "reward deficiency syndrome" and other genetic malfunctions (Chapter 1).
2. Extrinsic (environmental) factors portrayed as an unhealthy lifestyle associated largely with drug-plagued environment, PTSD, personal indiscipline, poverty, victims of broken or family dysfunction/neglect, and/or bad peer group influence.

Mental illness profoundly aggravates the vulnerability to drug addiction in a drug permissive environment or peer group. Drug addiction secondary to mental illness is often referred to as "dual diagnosis" (co-occurring disorder).

The "addicted brain" incorporates the abused psychoactive drug of choice into its normal physiology and/or psychology. This adaptation creates a physiological and/or psychological dependence and withdrawal symptoms are inevitable.

Long-term abuse causes the brain's chemical systems and circuits to change. A neurotransmitter, glutamate, enhances the reward circuit and learning ability. In the course of compromised production of glutamate as a result of drug abuse, cognitive function is consequently impaired.

Brain imaging studies of individuals suffering from drug addiction demonstrate changes in areas of the brain that are critical to judgment, decision-making, learning, memory, and behavior control. Besides the visible pathology, cravings of uncontrollable degree are often complications of drug abuse due to facilitation of conditioned learning. This occurs as an association of the drug of choice with person or place where they had the drug experience. This clinical evidence confirms drug addiction as a disease.

In a drug-plagued environment, people suffering from psychiatric disorders are highly predisposed to drug addiction and a combined illness of psychiatric disorders, and drug addiction is referred to as dual diagnosis or co-occurring disorder. It is essential to conduct a screening procedure for mental illness as part of assessment protocol for a diagnosed addict. This would broaden the specific treatment horizon needed to effect a holistic treatment.

STDs, HIV, AIDS, and other deadly infections are often complications of substance abuse or drug addiction. Drug addicts are very often involved in risky behaviors such as indiscriminate sexual intercourse and prostitution. These desperate sources of finance are needed to feed a compulsive use of psychoactive drugs of choice. The compulsion to try to regain once-experienced euphoria and the avoidance of excruciating withdrawal symptoms are driving forces behind drug addiction. This is common with physical addiction to heroin as well as psychological cravings for cocaine.

In addition to unprotected sex, the use of infected hypodermic needles and other paraphernalia exposes drug abusers to HIV/AIDS, hepatitis C, and other blood-borne diseases and STDs, which can be potentially fatal. Harm-reduction strategies include information about risks, safe use of condoms, and access to sterile injection equipment (see "Harm Reduction" in Chapter 2). This can stop or minimize infection transmission.

Another disease caused by drug abuse and in particular heroin use is leukoencephalopathy, a disease that affects neurons surrounding the brain and spinal cord. Symptoms include mental confusion, vision damage, speech and coordination problems, paralysis, coma, and death.

Endocarditis is an infection of the inner lining of the heart. A common infection is by *Streptococcus viridian*, which can precipitate dysfunction of the cardiac valves and eventual cardiac failure and death. Infected hypodermic needles used in drug injection can spread this infection to other parts of the body.

5.10 Culture-Centered Treatment Program

The concern of alcoholism and drug addiction in society cannot be overemphasized. Stress, with all its causes and ramifications, is a significant extrinsic factor that can aggravate vulnerability to drug use. This treatment group is another therapy model that promotes a robust interaction within a cultural group that ensures a client's safety and trust with a goal to address and resolve stresses of intercultural misperception, dispel myths, and encourage healthy lifestyles. As we know them, cultural beliefs, assumptions, myths, and prejudices are intricate fibers of our being. They sometimes bring out the best and worst in us. Thus, any cultural group may benefit from this culture-centered treatment approach. The intent is not to introduce racial or cultural segregation to therapy, but rather to enlighten minds and enhance functioning and understanding in a diverse and complex world. It helps reduce stress especially with clients with these hang-ups and fosters long-term recovery. This is essential and productive especially to marginalized groups undergoing treatment. As a treatment response to these cultural complexities, the *"Cultural Bias" Treatment Model* is a cognition therapy concept and a product of my clinical experience. It is rooted in the principles of evidence-based practices such as reality/choice control therapy, CBT, and the spirituality of a 12-step program. It places cultural beliefs and influences on socialization under microscope. These include culture-oriented misinterpretations or conclusions that sometimes formulate dysfunctional childhood upbringing and life experiences. These life situations constitute the kind of stressors that may be the tipping point for vulnerable people to use and abuse drugs. Such aggravating stressors could present as depression, paranoia, delusions, and aggression tendencies, to mention a few. It also focuses on dealing with the realities of our society, employing a healthy approach that is open-minded, proactive, and self and family protective. Thus, the essence of "cultural bias" treatment model is to provide a safe environment for clients' disclosures and resolutions of these stressors and their etiologies that stymie treatment progression. The model provides a therapeutic forum for addressing these issues. It should be mentioned that cultural bias treatment group is one type of clinically informative behavior programs. Members are encouraged to participate in integrative (multicultural) treatment group programs.

Here is an experimental group therapy for Black/African Americans. The proposed clinicians are Black/African-American therapists. The primary goal is to facilitate discussion of culture-sensitive topics, adverse effects, and resolutions that promote healthy socio-cultural interaction. The facilitator must be an experienced behavioral therapist/counselor with expertise in multicultural studies. Acumen in recognizing the language and social setting of denial and rationalization, and applying appropriate intervention is important.

The interaction and conversation should be facilitated in a healthy environment of mutual trust, respect, and empathy. Discussions should promote individualized and group understanding of cultural diversity, which dispels off myths, addresses paranoia, with a goal of promoting stress reduction, and ultimately creates a positive influence on clients struggling with addiction.

5.11 Concept of the Model

- The Past and Closure
  Revisit the past and explore memories and flashbacks,
  Introspection on childhood and adulthood,
  Assessment of individual challenges and strengths,
  Resolution of issues of psychological and emotional trauma, and related dysfunctions,
  Spirituality as applicable,
  Come to terms with ancestral issues,
  Closure with deep understanding of all individual and group problems,
  Enhance self-esteem: positive impact on parenting, relationships, ancestry (DNA) related to past and present medical history of addiction, mental illness with education on treatments,
  The conversation about the past must be about both positive and difficult experiences and memories; this talk must be brief and resolved with closure.
- The Present (Here and Now)
  Reality of now—poverty, addiction, racism, disease, education,
  Gang mentality, homelessness, violence,
  Resolution of present problems and development of coping skills,

Socialization, attitude adjustment, anger management, and spirituality,
Resources and information provided to meet present needs and advancement toward a secured future,
Programs targeting self-care, treatments, individual responsibility,
Concept of addiction,
Treatment options best suited for effective recovery and maintenance of recovery.
*   The Future
Recovery/Sobriety as a continuum with coping skills, tools for maintaining recovery,
Spirituality as applicable to resolution.

The implementation of this model will need to be concurrent with other modalities of treatment as relevant to individual problems such as pharmacotherapy and psychotherapy that are evidence-based practices as specified in a treatment plan. The model could also be applied to other cultural groups in the community.

I facilitated an African-American group that appears to share my philosophy of a culture-centered treatment approach. Here is an interactive experience with case studies. Names are fictitious for confidentiality purposes.

Case Study: Leroy's Lifetime Frustration (From Author's Clinical Diary)

This was a group of African-American men and women, with mutual determination to a self-oriented, inward search. They strove to eliminate cultural and individual barriers against alcoholism and addiction treatment. This approach promotes a continuum of treatment to guarantee lifelong recovery. In prior sessions we guaranteed the presence of an unspoken but strong bond of trust, empathy, respect, un-alienated interaction, and commitment to the goals of the group.

It was Leroy's turn to check in. The process involves addressing the group about his situation, problems, and strengths. A striking comment he made took everyone by surprise, "I hate white people."

There was a brief period of introspective silence after which I responded, "It's a good thing that you can share your feelings and frustrations. Our goal is to have an open conversation and come to a resolution beneficial to you and everyone else in the group. Are you comfortable receiving feedback from other members?"

"Yes," he affirmed. Leroy was a 55-year-old man. He was, at the time, attending an anger-management program as well as an African-American group. He had spent over 20 years in incarceration for felonies that included recurrent use and peddling of illicit drugs. His goals were to complete anger control, achieve and maintain sobriety.

"Why do you hate white people?" I asked. And in response he delved into a litany of all the wrongs in his life that he claimed were caused by every Caucasian he had ever related with, from his nightmarish ex-wife who got him hooked on drugs to constant police harassment. The details of the conversation and closure were so protracted, they are worthy of another book.

I engaged him, however, with soul-searching questions. "Leroy, don't you think that declaring yourself as a victim is like giving your power away?"

After a thoughtful moment, he agreed that it was. I sensed that some understanding about his situation was gradually and slowly creeping into his cognition.

"Do you like all black people, Leroy?"

Here I presume he was stunned as well as humored by my question. In my direction, he cast a serious contemplative look that grew into a smile. "Not all of them," he confessed. "I love my mom, my uncles, and other relatives and friends that are always there for me."

"What about the gang members in your community?" I asked.

He seemed uncomfortable and hurriedly responded in utter disgust, "I hate them. My favorite nephew was a gang member. He was killed by them. I'd tried to warn him about the evil of gangs."

I expressed my condolences for his loss. I conducted a brief review of his current treatment regime, inclusive of anger management, psychotherapy, and present lifestyle choices.

I introduced a discussion on over-generalization as a distortion of thoughts and misperception of human behavior. It was the right moment to have a group discussion on prejudices and self-criticism which addresses bias and self-esteem respectively. It was a sincere and honest interaction, full of sharing of thoughts, beliefs, and misconceptions with revelation of individual bias or cognitive distortions that give rise to errors in judgment, behavior, and attitude. Also, over-generalization, mind reading, labeling of self-criticism according to D. D. Burns' "Triple-Column Technique" was a subject of discussion. It teaches rational response to automatic thoughts, boosting self-esteem.

Their genuineness in accepting responsibility for wrong assumptions and willingness to make a positive change is a first remarkable step toward cognitive restructuring. A repeated session of this form of cognitive exercise, encouraging clients' input from daily life experiences, enhances retention of behavior learning.

There was positive evidence of Leroy's behavior adjustment and consequent movement toward sobriety and anger control through his therapy sessions with me. These changes in Leroy's thought processes served to enhance rational cognition in his course of treatment, and had a positive impact on other members of the group.

This is the essence of this unique group. It provides a safe environment for clients' disclosures, reality checks, and resolution of daily stressors of false beliefs and conflicts in a therapeutic forum.

5.12 Al-Anon

This is a support group for friends and family of alcoholics and addicts. The Al-Anon family group unites the addict's loved ones with the common goal of resolving their own problems through the sharing of experiences, strengths, and hope. The group's concept is based on "12-step principles." These are intended to advance spiritual paradigm that empowers members to carry on. This conceptual framework helps provide the courage necessary for family members to support loved ones in navigating through the difficult process of dealing with drug addiction and treatment.

Al-Anon was formed in 1951 by Lois Wilson, the wife of Bill Wilson, Al-Anon's co-founder and the founder of AA. Lois Wilson came to understand the stressful situations associated with family members of alcoholics from her husband's struggle with alcoholism.

The family members often experience a dysfunctional dynamic with their addicted member(s) that involves control, codependence, manipulation, and guilt-feeling of being partly responsible for the addiction. The group attempts to promote transformation of low self-esteem, dejectedness, guilt-feeling, and hopelessness of family members and friends of alcoholics into a spiritual empowerment that assigns responsibility for these dysfunctions to a disease. This conviction is responsible for a change of heart that fosters kindness, forgiveness, and healthy and supportive interactions.

Al-Anon sponsors Alateen, a 12-step recovery program for young people affected by a loved one's drinking. Membership is open for teens aged 12–19.

Placement criteria are very relevant in the treatment of drug addiction. This is discussed in the follow-up. It also lends some insight to the discussion on "Levels of Care in Structured Programs" (see Section 6.3).

5.13 American Society of Addiction Medicine Patient Placement Criteria

Since the early 1990s, a treatment-matching scheme, American Society of Addiction Medicine Patient Placement Criteria (ASAM-PPC), has been developed by professionals who incorporate client evaluation for placement at an appropriate level of care.

This placement criteria allows a "clinician to systematically evaluate the severity of a patient's need for treatment along six dimensions and then utilize a fixed combination rule to determine which of four levels of care a substance abusing patient will respond with the greatest success" (Turner et al., 1999). The four levels of care are: outpatient treatment (Level 1); intensive outpatient/partial hospitalization (Level 2); medically monitored intensive inpatient treatment (Level 3); and medically managed intensive inpatient treatment (Level 4) (Kosanke et al., 2002).

This placement criterion is intended to arrest or minimize overtreatment (a complication of mismatches) and thereby redistribute resources with utmost efficacy. This level of efficiency could help to avoid under treatment and achieve a preferred and more appropriate level of care.

Bio-psycho-social clinical data on a patient is obtained by applying the six ASAM assessment dimensions to categorize the data.

Dimension 1: Intoxication/Withdrawal

Observation of patient's intoxication and reaction.
Frequency of drug intake or withdrawal symptoms.

Dimension 2: Biomedical conditions/complications

Current medication effect, complaints, and/or reaction to medication.

Dimension 3: Emotional/Behavioral/Cognitive: This is assessment of the complexity of problems including behavioral displays of anger or frustration, family discord, and other relevant causative factors. Assessment of the impulsive or compulsive behavior dynamics.

Dimension 4: Readiness to change: Willingness to communicate with therapist. Patient's account of incident if patient is cognitive.

Dimension 5: Relapse/continued use/continued problem potential

Patient's current state and predictability of prognosis.

Dimension 6: Recovery environment

Assessment of the patient's immediate environment.
Is it healthy and supportive to foster patient recovery?

The validity and effectiveness of ASAM-PPC is still in question because of contention over queried results from matches of dimensions and level of care placement. However, irrespective of this imperfection, the criteria have been, to a large extent, very useful tools in patient management. The concept is analogous to case management and serves two purposes: these tools can determine an individualized service plan for clients, guaranteeing utmost effectiveness. And this remediation makes sure that money disbursed on each client is wisely and most expeditiously spent.

5.14 HIPAA (Health Insurance Portability and Accountability Act) of 1996

The right to privacy and security of personal information of clients is essential to ensure their dignity and pride. The Office for Civil Rights (O.C.R) is responsible for enforcing HIPAA.

HIPAA privacy rule provides Federal protections for personal health information held by covered entities (Healthcare providers) and afford clients a spectrum of rights with respect to that information. At the same time, the privacy rule is I balanced so that it permits the disclosure of personal health information needed for clients' care and other important purposes.

HIPAA security rule is particularly specific of the series of administrative, physical and technical safeguards for covered entities to use to ensure the confidentiality, integrity and availability of electronic protected health information.

6 Pharmacotherapy (Medication Therapy)

Pharmacotherapy is a significant component in holistic management of alcoholism and drug addiction. This therapy uses active chemicals via prescription or herbal remedies for the treatment of neurochemical imbalances that are causative mechanisms or for alleviating signs and symptoms that impede recovery. Pharmacotherapy has, with scientific research, evolved to a level where scientists have designed new anticraving medications and abstinence-enhancing drugs for the management of chemical dependence.

6.1 Current Medication Management of Alcohol Dependence

Antabuse (Disulfiram) was the first medicine approved by the USFDA in the treatment of alcohol abuse. Alcohol is metabolized in the body through a toxic intermediate and a final harmless product.

$$\text{Alcohol} \rightarrow \underset{\text{Toxic product}}{\text{Acetaldehyde}} \rightarrow \text{Acetic acid}$$

The acetaldehyde accumulation causes many of the symptoms that heavy drinkers often experience. The symptoms range from mild to severe and could result in fatality. The function of Antabuse is to provide blockage of further oxidative breakdown of acetaldehyde in the body. This accelerates and elevates the toxic effect of acetaldehyde related to the severity of drinking while on Antabuse. Mild symptoms include flushing, nausea, copious vomiting, sweating, thirst, throbbing in the head and neck, headache, respiratory difficulty, chest pain, palpations, dyspnea, hyperventilation, tachycardia, weakness, hypotension, syncope, marked uneasiness, vertigo, blurred vision, and confusion.

Severe reactions are respiratory depression, cardiovascular collapse, myocardial infarction, acute congestive heart failure, unconsciousness, arrhythmias, convulsion, and death.

Antabuse functions solely as a physical and psychological deterrent to drinking. It is administered only to patients who have a full knowledge of the consequence of drinking while on the medication and are committed to stop drinking. Antabuse has other contraindications such as allergy to the medication, history of severe heart disease, psychosis, the use of paraldehyde or metronidazole, or in pregnancy.

Practical Skills and Clinical Management of Alcoholism and Drug Addiction.
DOI: http://dx.doi.org/10.1016/B978-0-12-398518-7.00006-7

Research in Europe, where Antabuse is more frequently used, has revealed that long-term use of Antabuse as an aversive agent is very effective in helping clients to stop drinking.

Naltrexone (opioid antagonist) is often marketed as its hydrochloride salt with trade names Revia and Depade. Vivitrol is an extended-release formulation sold in the United States.

Naltrexone functions as an antagonist in the management of alcohol and opioid dependence. Opioid-induced constipation, especially in patients with advanced illness, is treated with methylnatrexone bromide.

Naltrexone attempts to reduce the impact of the effects of alcohol-reinforcing stimuli. With the use of naltrexone, problem drinkers have reported less "alcohol highs." Social drinkers taking naltrexone report less positive and more sedative and unpleasant effects from alcohol (King, Volpicelli, Frazer, & O'Brien, 1997). Reduced craving for alcohol is observed among both social and problem drinkers when on naltrexone. Disulfiram and naltrexone require client compliance in order to be effective.

Acamprosate: Under the trade name of Campral, acamprosate is used in treating alcohol dependence. The substance is assumed to effectively stabilize chemical balances in the brain which are otherwise vulnerable to disruption by the effect of alcohol. The process involves blocking glutamatergic N-methyl-D-aspartate (NMDA) receptors while gamma-aminobutyric acid type-A receptors are activated. The effectiveness of acamprosate is ensured when patients attend support groups and abstain from alcohol. Side effects include allergic reactions, irregular heartbeats, raised or lowered blood pressure, headaches, insomnia, and impotence. Acamprosate is contraindicated in patients with kidney problems or in clients who are allergic to the medication.

6.2 Drug Detoxification and Maintenance Treatment

This method of crisis intervention is not a complete treatment process, but rather a pharmacotherapeutic treatment often referred to as medically assisted treatment that paves the way for further treatment procedures such as counseling and psychosocial support, reflected in support group programs. This is essential for holistic management and recovery. Drug detoxification is the first step in drug treatment, followed by maintenance dosing that could be lifelong, a few years, or several months as in methadone, suboxone, or other treatment programs. The clinical application of a detoxification drug may last 2–7 days or as long as 2 weeks or more in cases with severe withdrawal symptoms.

The detoxification and maintenance period is complemented with structured programs of behavior-based therapy delivered with evidence-based practices and peer support that promote behavior modification and positive lifestyle, enhancing treatment success.

Methadone (Dolophine): This highly effective therapeutic medicine serves to rehabilitate clients suffering from heroin, morphine, and other opioid drug addiction, who are in the process of detoxification. Methadone is a synthetic opioid receptor full agonist, employed in the treatment of heroin and other opioid-dependent addictions. It is effective due to its analgesic action and suppression of withdrawal symptoms. Its anticraving action involves the stabilization of the dysregulated neurotransmitters in the brain related to intense heroin craving. The drug is orally administered or infused into the blood.

Methadone displaces opiates from the receptors of natural painkillers termed endorphins. Methadone dampens the "high" from heroin and does not provide such a euphoric rush. Some patients dispute this claim; for example, a patient with chronic myelogenous leukemia claims the analgesic effect of methadone comes with a profound euphoria.

Besides its craving-depletion effect, it has a longer lifespan than heroin, an advantage that reduces the frequency of administration of methadone. It is regulated and monitored in the course of treatment because of its addictive effect.

The side effects of methadone administration are constipation, drowsiness, blurred vision, clumsiness of movement, extremely dry mouth, flushing, headache, nausea, and vomiting. Heroin rapid detox, rapid detoxification from high-tolerance heroin use, must be avoided because it can be extremely dangerous or fatal.

Methadone Clinics

The establishment of methadone clinics has contributed immensely to the treatment of opiate drug addiction. This medication-assisted treatment complex includes methadone as a drug addiction detoxification and as a maintenance medication. Patients may stay on methadone for several months to a few years. Some benefit from lifelong treatment.

The maintenance period is coupled with psychosocial counseling and peer support that helps clients learn to recognize the situations, feelings, or events that could trigger a desire to abuse opioids. The recognition of these triggers in oneself and the world around one, and learning new coping skills, can help to avoid triggers or to manage them as they happen.

The medication dosing instruction must be strictly followed to avoid serious side effects or death due to respiratory depression. It must be kept in a secure place not accessible to others to avoid the risk of wrongful use. Unpleasant withdrawal symptoms could result from abrupt cessation of intake.

Contraindications

Use of alcohol, alcohol content in medication, or other CNS depressants such as diazepines is contraindicated while on methadone. Dangerous side effects or death due to respiratory depression may result from synergistic effects of drug interaction.

Allergy to opiates such as codeine, morphine, Oxycontin, Darvocet, Vicodin, Lortab, and so forth can occur. Asthma attack and bowel obstruction (paralytic ileus) are contraindications.

In pregnancy or during a breastfeeding period, methadone in breast milk is harmful, causing neonatal addiction and withdrawal symptoms or precipitating fatal respiratory depression.

Consultation with a doctor is advised in:

- Asthma, COPD, sleep apnea, or other breathing disorders,
- Renal or liver disease,
- Abnormal curvature of the spine,
- History of head injury or brain tumor,
- Epilepsy or other seizure disorder,
- Low blood pressure,
- Gallbladder disease,
- Underactive thyroid,
- Enlarged prostate, urination problems,
- Addison disease or other adrenal gland disorders,
- Mental illness,
- History of alcoholism and drug addiction,
- Older adults and people with debilitating condition because of sensitivity to methadone.

Buprenorphine (Buprenex), marketed under the brand names Subutex and Suboxone, is a semisynthetic opiate with partial agonist action at the μ-opioid receptor. This powerful analgesic is administered sublingually (under the tongue) in a high-dosage pill to enhance rapid effect in the management of opioid addiction. Its uniqueness is its "partial agonist" effect. This has a plateau effect at specific critical dosage that ensures safety. Buprenorphine is less likely to be abused than a full agonist such as methadone. This safety factor means this agent can be easily prescribed by a trained physician on an outpatient basis, unlike methadone, which is more controlled.

Suboxone as Opiate Addiction Treatment

Suboxone in the form of suboxone sublingual film and suboxone sublingual tablets are addiction treatment medications. They can cause serious life-threatening respiratory depression and death, particularly when taken by intravenous route in combination with benzodiazepines or other CNS depressants such as sedatives, tranquilizers, or alcohol. Dose reduction of the combinations should be considered, and liver function should be monitored before and during treatment because cytolytic hepatitis, jaundice, and allergic reactions including anaphylactic shock have been reported. Neonatal withdrawal has also been reported when used in pregnancy or during breastfeeding. It must be kept out of reach of children because they suffer fatal respiratory depression if exposed to the medication.

Adverse effects commonly observed with suboxone treatment include headache, nausea, vomiting, sweating, constipation, signs and symptoms of withdrawal, insomnia, pain, swelling of the limbs, disturbance of attention, palpitation, and blurred vision. Thus, caution must be taken when driving vehicles or operating hazardous machinery.

Stages of Treatment: Steps in medically assisted treatment with buprenorphine (suboxone sublingual film). The suboxone sublingual film is available in two strengths:

2 mg buprenorphine with 0.5 mg naloxone and
8 mg buprenorphine with 2 mg naloxone.

Induction: This is the commencement of medication treatment. Buprenorphine ONLY is used for induction, and suboxone sublingual film is prescribed as maintenance dose.

Maintenance: This involves clinical monitoring by a doctor and recommendation of counseling and psychosocial support. While the treatment medication suppresses withdrawal and reduces craving, counseling and peer support equip clients with tools to identify high-risk situations that may trigger relapse and have coping mechanisms in place, creating positive behavior, and making meaningful lifestyle changes.

Medical Taper: It is ultimately the decision of the patient and the health care team when they determine the time is right to slowly taper or step down the dose of suboxone sublingual film.

Achieving Effective Counseling of Opiate-Addicted Patients

Group Counseling

This is uniquely effective in the treatment of opioid dependence because it provides a support network fostered by peer support and acceptance that presents a family-like environment. This warm and receptive environment nurtures improved self-esteem, security, hope, and purpose where patients learn from real-world examples of other people experiencing recovery, and also receive positive feedback to help improve their self-image, which is the ultimate goal of therapy.

Individual Therapy

In a private session with counselors, mental health issues such as depression, anxiety, and psychosis are conditions of vulnerability to drug addiction that are better addressed and treated in this therapeutic format.

Group Programs

These aftercare programs are mostly abstinence based and offer psychosocial support to patients struggling with drug addiction as well as strengthening patients in recovery. It is most often a lifelong supportive exercise that assists clients with maintenance of sobriety and recovery.

The peer support is similar to group counseling without the guidance and facilitation of a professional counselor. The concept is that people who suffer from a similar problem understand and can help one another. Regular meetings that provide an avenue for robust interaction where people who are in recovery can help guide others out of addiction. NA is one of many of these programs.

Naloxone Hydrochloride (Narcan): This longer-acting opioid full antagonist is a synthetic compound structurally congruent with oxymorphone. Narcan injection is available as a sterile preparation for intravenous, intramuscular, and subcutaneous administration. The substance is indicated for complete or partial reversal of opioid and respiratory depression induced by natural and synthetic opioids: methadone, propoxyphane, and certain agonist–antagonist analgesics including nalbuphine, pentazocine, butorphanol, and cyclazocine. This medication is indicated for diagnosis of acute opioid overdose. This remediation can be useful as an adjunctive agent in elevating blood pressure during management of septic shock.

Nalorphine (N-*allyl-normorphine*), with trade names Lethidrone and Nalline, acts at two opioid receptor sites. At the μ-receptor, this substance acts as an antagonist and at the κ-receptor site as an agonist. This substance is used in reversing opioid overdose.

Rapid Opiate Detoxification Under Anesthesia (RODA): This is a procedure of withdrawing from opiates (heroin, opium, codeine, methadone, etc.). It is only a small part of a more comprehensive addiction treatment program that includes behavior-based therapy. It is a service best provided to those who cannot tolerate withdrawal symptoms. It is a significant impediment to abstinence-based recovery.

Clients seeking RODA must be actively engaged in a program of recovery prior to the procedure. The process is preceded by assessment of the client: present and past medical history, family history, screening for drug allergies and other conditions that may be contraindicated. It is followed by a detoxification procedure which lasts about 8 h.

Levomethadyl Acetate (USAN), or LAAM (trade name), Levacetylmethadol (INN), or Levo-Alpha-Acetyl Methadol (LAAM) is a synthetic opioid. It bears a structural similarity to methadone and is employed as a substitute for methadone in the treatment of opioid dependence. This medication's lifespan during opioid detox surpasses that of methadone. This substance is administered three times a week and thus offers the convenience of fewer trips to the hospital. There are no apparent withdrawal symptoms, but there is evidence of the life-threatening complication of cardiac arrhythmia.

This remediation should be reserved for use in the treatment of opiate-addicted patients who fail to respond adequately to other medications. LAAM should be administered with extreme care to patients prone to prolonged QT syndrome as in congestive heart failure, cardiac hypertrophy, bradycardia, diuretic use, hypomagnesemia, or hypokalemia. It is contraindicated in prolonged QT values (greater than 430 in males or greater than 450 in females) observed on electrocardiogram monitoring equipment.

LAAM was approved in 1993 by the USFDA. In 2003, Roxane Laboratories, Inc. discontinued LAAM production in the United States. In 2001, LAAM was removed from the European market due to the report of life-threatening cardiac complications (ventricular rhythm disorders) (Wolstein et al., 2009).

6.3 Levels of Care in Structured Programs

This provides therapeutic services which include individual and group psychotherapy, psychiatric medication management, exercise therapy, acupuncture, massage, nutrition counseling, meditation, yoga, biofeedback, and drug and alcohol testing. The application of these services in appropriate therapeutic dose to meet the adequate treatment of these different levels of care is the goal of this discussion.

The essential clinical approach employed in ensuring ultimate treatment is the ASAM-PPC. This serves as the compatibility match for the placement of clients into an appropriate level of care as discussed in Section 5.13.

The four levels of care are as follows:

1. Outpatient treatment
2. Intensive outpatient/partial hospitalization
3. Medically monitored intensive outpatient treatment
4. Medically managed intensive inpatient treatment.

A detailed discussion of these levels of care, admission, program, and provider criteria is presented in the following discussion.

Outpatient Program

This program has less need for structure compared to an intensive program, but still provides assistance with client addiction, including methadone maintenance programs on a weekly basis. In addition to these centers, other facilities may provide for specific needs of clients.

Inpatient/Residential Treatment Program

This is a live-in treatment facility with daily structured programs for residents. Their participation ranges between 6 and 12h in a 24-h period. The structure may involve individual, group, and/or family counseling taking the form of educational, vocational, nutritional, and spiritual programs with supportive AA or NA meetings three to seven times per week. This could also be conducted at penal institutions, or psychiatric or general hospitals.

Intensive Outpatient Program

An intensive structured program of 2–3h per session, 3–5 days per week on an outpatient basis. This includes individual, group, and/or family counseling. This primarily focuses on education, vocation, nutrition, and spirituality while encouraging participation in ongoing programs such as AA and NA.

The program is structured to meet the needs of intensive inpatient and outpatient programs in consideration of affordability for some clients.

Medically Monitored Intensive Inpatient Treatment/Program (Adult ASAM Level II.7)

Federal Chapter (79-09.1-04) gives clear definitions of provider programs and admission criteria. The definition (75-09.1-04-01) states that *" 'medically monitored intensive inpatient treatment' means a substance abuse treatment program that provides a planned regimen of twenty-four-hour professionally directed evaluation and observation. This includes medical monitoring and addiction treatment in an inpatient setting. The program is appropriate for clients whose sub-acute detoxification, withdrawal, biomedical, and emotional, behavioral, or cognitive problems are so severe that they require inpatient treatment but do not need the full resources of an acute care general hospital or a medically managed inpatient treatment program."*

Provider criteria (75-09.1-04-02). The program shall *"offer twenty-four-hour skilled nursing care, daily onsite counseling services, and a physician's services twenty-four hours per day seven days per week. This program shall make available specialized professional consultation and offer inpatient treatment programs seven days per week, with the length of stay to be determined by a client's condition and functioning."*

Program criteria (75-09.1-04-03). A medically monitored intensive inpatient treatment program shall provide *"a combination of individual and group therapy as deemed appropriate by an assessment and treatment plan. Medical and nursing services available onsite to provide ongoing assessment and care of acute detoxification needs, medical, and psychiatric problems. A system for referral of clients for identified treatment needs if the service is not available in the program. Family treatment services as deemed appropriate by an assessment and treatment plan; and educational and informational programming adapted to individual client needs."*

Admission criteria (75-09.1-04-04). *"Before a medically monitored intensive inpatient program may admit a client, the client shall meet diagnostic criteria for a substance dependence disorder of the DSM and meet specifications in at least two of the six ASAM dimensions. At least one of these must be dimension one, two, or three in the following criteria:"*

> *"The client is experiencing signs and symptoms of acute withdrawal, there is evidence that severe withdrawal is imminent, or there is a strong likelihood that the client will not complete detoxification at another level of care and enter continued treatment or self-help recovery;*
> *The client has a physical condition or complication impacting immediate safety or well-being;*
> *The client has a psychiatric condition or complication impacting immediate safety or well-being;*
> *The client exhibits severe impairment in a significant life area: legal, family, or work;*
> *The client exhibits significant loss or control and relapse symptoms; or*
> *The client has had multiple attempts at treatment programs of lower intensity with an inability to stay sober."*

History: Effective October 26, 2004.
Law Implemented: NDCC 50-31.

Medically Managed Intensive Inpatient Treatment/Program (Level IV)

This service is often delivered as adolescent Level IV treatment, an acute inpatient care. This care provides 24-h medically coordinated assessment and treatment provided by a professional team of doctors, nurses, and other relevant professionals who are addiction medicine experts. The acute biomedical, emotional, behavioral, and cognitive forms of chemical substance dependence disorders clinically presented will dictate immediate treatment response. This remediation meets specifications in ASAM dimensions D1, D2, and D3. The service duration is a function of the prognosis. The program reflects conditions or protocols that safeguard procedures.

Assessment and Referral Programs: These programs are patient placement centers that conduct evaluations which recommend the most appropriate facilities for patients.

Education Programs: An educational process that offers knowledge concerning health risks to patients who experience minimal problems with psychoactive drug use.

Transition Program: This is an intermediate state between completion of intensive inpatient and independent living. The program provides basic shelter, food, counseling, and other services. These are halfway houses and supported housing facilities. Their goal is to prepare clients for independent living.

It is important to note the differences between these programs or treatment modalities. It is critical to realize that effective treatment often requires the services of two or more modalities to assist in the recovery process. A continuum of care enhances optimum success for recovery maintenance.

The study of causes of drug addiction and treatment is a subject of continued research. No matter how it is approached, the complex interaction of intrinsic and extrinsic factors influencing the causes and challenges to treatment procedures requires ongoing research and investigation. Knowledge is contemporary, and research studies have always been the vehicle to ultimate treatment progress. Genetic defect therapy is the follow-up subject of clinical study.

6.4 "Replacement" Theory

The concept of polygenic (multiple alleles) cause for addiction was described by E. Comings, MD, Director of the Department of Medical Genetics at City of Hope Medical Center in Duarte, California. This therapy validates the existence of single gene (allele) and polygenic (multiple alleles) variances. Treatment of reward deficiency syndrome (as in phenotype of A1 variance of D_2 D_3 D_4 D_5 genes that result in reduced dopamine receptors) theoretically would indicate need for a dopamine source to impact drug abuse or addiction. In replacement therapy of A1 variance, bromocriptine would be the drug treatment of choice. Treatment would require an individual genetic profile evaluation through molecular biogenetic studies. This genome study would provide insight into defective phenotypes and appropriate medication replacements that might include bromocriptine in variance A1.

6.5 Ibogaine Therapy

Ibogaine is a naturally occurring psychoactive substance extracted from the roots of a plant (shrub) called Iboga. Iboga (*Tabernanthe iboga*) is classified as a member of the Apocynaceae family. This is the richest source for Ibogaine, an indole alkaloid.

Iboga plants are common vegetation that extends from Cameroon to the Congo in the tropical heat and humidity of Africa. But Gabon, one of the countries along the coast of Africa, is where Iboga grows best. The *Tabernanthe manii* root also contains

Ibogaine as one of several alkaloids. In West Africa, *Voacanga agricana* is a widespread shrub containing Ibogaine in its bark. In Australia, *Ervatamia orientalis* produces Ibogaine in its leaves. And in South America, a shrub called *Anartia meyer*, found in Trinidad and Tobago, Venezuela, Colombia, Surinam, and French Guyana, has been discovered to contain Ibogaine.

Ibogaine's unique psychoactive effect defies predictable clinical manifestations. For centuries, the sacred root of the Iboga has been used in medicinal and ritual preparations according to African spiritual traditions of the Bwiti of Gabon in a personal quest for knowledge and inner power, a shamanic aspiration. The Nganga African tribe traditionally uses Iboga to treat mental illnesses including depression, anxiety, and even schizophrenia.

When Ibogaine is administered, the visionary phase comes first. This is described as a lucid or active dream that extends from 4 to 6 h. This visual phenomenon is an awakening dream state without loss of consciousness. This state produces brain waves characteristic of REM sleep and has been characterized as a recreation of fetal sleep. It is documented that this produces instructive replays of life events that led to addiction.

During the introspection phase, Ibogaine promotes psychotherapeutic effect that empowers the client to conquer fear and negative emotions that may drive their addictions. This phase allows clients to explore psychological issues and behavior patterns that support addictions and other psychological problems. Hallucinogenic and euphoric actions of psychoactive drugs normally graduate into a state of "dependency" when addiction is established. This would be the case with LSD "trips" and flashbacks. But Ibogaine's unique psychoactivities, which are the hallucinogenic and introspective phases, are utilized as individual "therapy" that is focused, devoid of euphoria and dependency. This hallucinogenic experience or vision was characterized by *"Narranjo, a psychiatrist who studied ibogaine and harmaine as oneirophrenics or dream makers from the Greek oneiros, 'dream' and phren 'think' as opposed to hallucinogens. French researchers (Goutarel, Gollnhofer and Sillans) have suggested that iboga (Ibogaine) allows people to disconnect the 'self' from the external reality in order to reconnect themselves to an inner reality, while still being able at any time to return to what is happening around them"* (Ravalec, Mallendi, & Paicheler, 2007).

Studies indicate that Ibogaine interrupts addiction and diminishes or eradicates cravings and withdrawal symptoms. All research conducted arrived at clinical affirmations that Ibogaine therapy can put an end to physical and psychological dependence, as well as terminate withdrawal symptoms of addictions to psychoactive drugs and alcoholism.

Pharmacology and Pharmacokinetics of Ibogaine

Ibogaine has unique and complex pharmacological properties, including a broad spectrum of binding on receptors sites as an agonist (hallucinogenic) and antagonist (antiaddictives). This reflects its peculiar clinical characteristics. The primary target sites are the NMDA, nicotinic, σ-, κ-opioid, and μ-receptors. NMDA are receptors of the messengers of glutamate, calcium, aspartate, amino acid, and glycine. Glutamate is noted to be the most important neurotransmitter booster of the CNS. The glutamate neurons are the major neuronal transmitting network of the cortex, modulating cognition, hippocampus (memory), and amygdalas (emotion). These are essential for mental functions that preserve our daily existence.

Ibogaine acts on these multiple transmitter sites in an antagonist function as a "reducing agent," mitigating "excitotoxic damage in the brain." This is the apparent mechanism of action in effecting the antiaddictive process. Its application for "neuropathic pain" or treatment of Parkinson disease and Alzheimer disease is a possible future use.

The proposal for therapeutic use is worthy of clinical trials. Women are much more sensitive to Ibogaine than men, thus care must be taken in dose measurement to avoid overdose or fatality. Ibogaine could be a future "wonder drug" if patented as an antineurotoxic medication.

Molecular Level of Activities: The drug is a noncompetitive antagonist for $\alpha3\beta4$ nicotinic receptors. Other $\alpha3\beta4$ antagonists such as bupropion (Welbutrin or Zyban) and mecamylamine have been used in treatment of nicotine addiction. A combination of Ibogaine and other $\alpha3\beta4$ antagonists such as 18-MC, dextromethorphan, or mecamylamine have a stronger antiaddictive effect than Ibogaine administered alone. Ibogaine's antagonist actions on opioid and glutamatergic systems can be effective as antiaddictive functions within an hour of administration. Ibogaine is also a serotonin 5-HT2A, 5-HT2C, and $\sigma2$ receptor agonists. This is most probably responsible for its hallucinogenic effects.

Noribogaine (12-hyrdoxyibogamine) is a major metabolic product of Ibogaine. Ibogaine is metabolized in the human body by cytochrome P450 2D6. Noribogaine is very potent as a serotonin reuptake inhibitor and also acts as a full agonist of moderate κ- and weak μ-opioid receptors. This substance can displace opiates in a similar fashion as methadone. The agonist action of Noribogaine, especially at the κ-opioid receptor, contributes to the psychoactive effect of Ibogaine intake.

Ibogaine exhibits relatively low potency at its target sites. It is used at a dosage of 5 mg/kg body weight in minor treatment, and up to 30 mg/kg in intense polysubstance addiction management. Based on rat studies, it is probable that high doses may cause adverse side effects. When animals were subjected to 50 mg/kg, one-third developed neurodegeneration. A dosage of 75 mg/kg caused all of the rats to show a characteristic pattern of Purkinje neuron degeneration, primarily in the cerebellum. A dosage of 10–20 mg/kg is recommended as a safe dosage (with minimal neurotoxicity) in the treatment of addiction.

A single treatment has a healing effect that lasts 2–3 years. But some individuals require a second or third treatment session over a period of 12–18 months. Intensive counseling therapy and aftercare is critical during the interruption periods for effective treatment.

Side effects observed immediately on administration of large dose of Ibogaine include ataxia (difficult coordination of muscles in motion), xerostomia (dry mouth), followed by nausea, and vomiting. These symptoms may last between 4 and 24 h. Ibogaine may be given by enema to avoid the vomiting that causes loss of medication dose. Psychiatric medications are contraindicated because of adverse interaction with Ibogaine.

Ventricular ectopy could present with low ventricular ejection fraction which is a hallmark of systolic heart failure. It has been observed in a minority of patients during Ibogaine therapy. QT-interval prolongation and ventricular tachycardia after large dose was reported in the *New England Journal of Medicine*. Clinical supervision of the use of Ibogaine in treatment of addiction is highly recommended, while self-treatment should be discouraged because of adverse side effects that could result in fatality.

Global Use: At present, Ibogaine use for the treatment of addiction is prohibited in the United States. Ibogaine is classified like heroin as a schedule I substance. In 1994, Deborah Mash, PhD, received FDA authorization to conduct experimental treatments. Ibogaine is legally recognized in the United Kingdom, France, and Germany.

Ibogaine use is legal in Canada. In 2002, Marc Emery opened the Iboga Therapy House in Vancouver, Canada. The therapy house offers Ibogaine treatments with blood monitoring and electrocardiogram, complemented with posttreatment follow-up.

Ibogaine is legal in Mexico as well. "Awakening in the Dream House" is an integrative Ibogaine addiction therapy center in Mexico. The author's conversation with Rocky Caravelli, the manager of the therapy center, focused on side effect management to prevent or minimize fatalities. He disclosed that a "safe therapeutic dose and clinical monitoring are the essence of a successful treatment."

6.6 Nutrition and Recovery

One of the severe consequences of addiction is malnutrition. There is evidence that addicts often suffer nutritional deficiencies of amino acids, vitamins, carbohydrates, fats, antioxidants, and immunological complexes that are vital to essential body activities.

A balanced diet is critical to recovery and maintenance. This ensures the growth of healthy tissues and muscles. A balanced diet replenishes the damaged neurological system that eventually restores stable coordination of reflexes and cognition. In order to maximize the effects of nutrition, exercise helps the body more effectively to process nutrients. Healthy nutrition and exercise can be part of a healthy lifestyle that restores addicts to physical, mental, and psychological well-being and reduces cravings for drugs of choice. Referral to nutrition experts is best. The nutritional deficiencies caused by alcoholism and drug addiction and the essential vital nutritional replenishments are worth examining in detail. A balanced diet that is culturally compatible and affordable for the individual is best. Good diet can profoundly affect mood. Research has revealed that a balanced diet of high protein, carbohydrates, essential fats, and vitamin supplements has a positive impact in mitigating addictive cravings and enhancing health. The replenishment of the neurological system with amino acids, folic acid, and vitamin B complex has been shown to stabilize mood and minimize mood swings that are common in alcoholism and drug addiction. Tyrosine is a precursor to neurotransmitters norepinephrine and dopamine. These are chemical messengers that ensure mental alertness and efficacy. They are found in protein-rich foods like meat, poultry, and seafood. Tryptophan is essential in the production of serotonin, a chemical messenger required for sleep that creates a calming effect. Sources of tryptophan are bananas, milk, sunflower seeds, and turkey meat.

A new study in rats has found that *N*-acetylcysteine (NAC), a commonly available and generally nontoxic amino acid derivative, reverses changes in the brain's circuitry associated with cocaine. This is carried out by reversing cocaine-induced brain cells transformation (Moussawi et al., 2009).

Chains of amino acids that constitute essential protein are critically needed for neurological repair and body building to restore physical and mental health during the process of recovery.

Damage to the liver, pancreas, heart, circulation system, kidneys, CNS, hypothalamus, hair, skin, stomach, intestines, and mucus membranes are gradually replenished with a balanced diet of varieties of rich sources of protein, carbohydrates, essential fats, and supplements of vitamins at the early onset of recovery. The continuity of this healthy nutritional lifestyle combined with regular and adequate exercise during and posttreatment period is a significant driving force among other essential factors that foster sobriety and maintain recovery.

6.7 Combating Alcoholism with Nutrition

Alcoholism is a devastating mental and physical disease often rooted in the genes and activated by the effect of alcohol in the biochemistry of brain and body. It damages both mind and body. The current conventional management which is primarily a psychological treatment platform carries a relapse rate of 80%. Also, alcohol and drug addiction undermines physical health and mental stability by altering the desire for healthy nutrition and vitamins essential for their maintenance. A reversal of this damage on the body's delicate internal chemistry is feasible by placing the client undergoing addiction treatment on a complementary balanced nutrition and essential vitamin regime.

The body accommodates this disease through this following vicious pathway. The state of hypoglycemia—shakiness, mood swings, irritability, emotional instability, sudden fatigue, mental confusion—is triggered by insulin reaction to hyperglycemia precipitated by excess alcohol (sugar) consumption. This cycle is driven by compulsive alcohol intake. The resulting mood swings, elation (hyperglycemia), which is indicated by pleasure feelings from sudden surge of energy, and depression (hypoglycemia), reflective of guilt and shame, is evident of brain chemistry that alternates in an unstable state in response to serum nutrient concentration variability. These dysfunctional dynamics often cascade into endocrine fluctuation that could result in exhaustion.

Thus, it is not surprising that alcoholism constitutes a disturbance to a healthy nutrition pattern of the client. It impacts the body's nutritional processing to preserve mechanisms that propagate itself, as discussed earlier. All the signs and symptoms caused by disturbed metabolic cycle, as earlier enumerated, is evidence that alcoholism is not primarily a psychological disorder, but a complex dynamic of neurochemical dysfunction, nutritional, and vitamin deficiency. No amount of psychological counseling alone could talk an alcoholic out of nutritional distress. Failure to restore a balanced nutrition that nourishes the neurological and biochemical systems of the body may result in psychological masking that stand in the way of progress in treatment procedures.

Awareness through education is of immense significance. When a client understands addiction in the way that diabetes is a physiological disorder, he/she is cognizant of "dos and don'ts" essential in the disease management. The self-knowledge and insight open the gate to self-acceptance, self-confidence, less confusion, less feeling of guilt and shame, and a sense of purpose and commitment to treatment that welcome a comprehensive approach.

Case Study: Couple's Struggle with Alcoholism (From Author's Clinical Diary)

At the end of an alcohol and drug (A&D) group I facilitated, a couple that attended the session approached me, requesting for an appointment for a private counseling meet. I suggested referring them to a family therapist for the best intervention. They insisted on having at least a session with me if I didn't mind. I scheduled a session for the following week. At the session, the primary complaint was the couple's struggle with the wife's alcoholism that was complicated by nightly sleeplessness, compulsive consumption of alcohol, sweets, and ice cream that relieved her periodic headache and turned on her pleasure feeling. These regular nocturnal activities took a great toll on the husband. He was often exhausted at work. He added, "The saddest moment of my life is always on my way home from work. I dread it." His wife, shocked and disappointed, responded, "I know I have this problem, but I thought you love me!" "Yes, I do," he replied, "That's why I come home. But I'm always unhappy to find you inebriated whenever I get home." Family history revealed her father and uncle died of complications of alcoholism. She lost her mother to ovarian cancer. No eventful history on the husband's family. His parents are still alive and well. It was a session of revealing moment on both sides. In spite of the situation, they seemed to agree to face this challenge in unison. They both agreed to my referral to a family therapist and nutritionist. They attended and actively participated in the A&D counseling meeting and AA support group for over a year. They gave me a report of progress in the treatment and how their relationship was gradually undergoing a healing process.

6.8 Relapse Prevention

The essence of holistic management of alcoholism and drug addiction is to prevent or minimize relapse. The present low percentage of success in treatment reflects partly on risk of maintenance of sobriety and recovery of individuals. Many success stories have experienced warning signs that triggered one or more relapse incidents. Identification of these signs in the earliest development, followed by immediate, appropriate, and adequate response is crucial for preventing relapse.

Flare-up of causative or vulnerability factors or synergistic effect of interaction of these factors that precipitate alcoholism and addiction often destabilize sobriety maintenance equilibrium. Evidence of this scenario is acute emotional stress in loss or grief or sudden surge of psychiatric symptoms that are devastating, resulting in relapse. Earliest individual request for immediate medical treatment will be critical in effecting relapse prevention.

Psychological relapse begins well in advance before physical relapse. It is a thought or validation of drinking or drugging before it ever happens, while physical relapse is the act of taking that first drink of alcohol or first use of drug after being deliberately clean and sober for a period of time. Also, it is a unique individual experience related to his/her diagnosis and personal plan of recovery. Sometimes, following 30–90 days of sobriety, the maintenance process becomes challenging. It is not uncommon for a person to withdraw, isolate, and become fearful of the recovery process. Failure to reach out could result in relapse. Following are some relapse indicators.

6.9 Relapse Factors with Warning Signs and Triggers

- Refusal to use prescribed medication in medical model of management of vulnerable factors,
- Hanging out at the same old drinking or drugging spot,
- Keeping alcohol bottles, containers, syringes, needles, and drug paraphernalia around for whatever reason,
- Preoccupied thought of use of alcohol and/or drug,
- Overestimation of self-coping capabilities,
- Failure to abide with treatment plan, not keeping doctors' appointments, and evading therapy,
- Avoiding support groups of fellowship and entrenching in self-isolation,
- Flare-up of psychiatric illness,
- Lack of structure in life,
- Unrealistic goal setting: being too hard on self,
- Overwhelmed by stress: emotional, psychological, and physical,
- Preoccupation with resentment, unresolved issues, anger,
- Obsessive-compulsive disorder,
- Refusal to deal with reality of life: denial, delusion,
- Abrupt life changes: loss, grief, conflict,
- Irregular eating and sleeping patterns; energy level and personal hygiene,
- Difficulties in relationship: spouse still drinking or drugging,
- In denial of warning, signs and triggers of relapse.

In the early stage of recovery, past lifestyle use of alcohol and/or drugs frequently revisits in thoughts and dreams. The temptation to break abstinence often hangs in the corner of our mind. But a strong commitment to a daily treatment plan and support group meetings, in the course of time, offer self-awareness, self-confidence, and self-empowerment that help to mitigate cravings, relapse dreams, and uncertainties of early recovery. This healthy lifestyle enhances maintenance of sobriety and recovery.

In an effort to maintain recovery, revision of causes of relapse is vital. For example, effective and consistent management of psychiatric illness is critical and serves as a stabilization factor in dual diagnosis treatment. Other relapse factors, as applicable to an individual, must be adequately addressed, encouraging individual responsibility in adhering to conditions that support relapse prevention.

It is proactive to cultivate a culture of relapse prevention by identifying behavior, exposure, or objects that put an individual at risk and employ recovery tools to break the cycle.

A periodic review of relapse prevention plan of individual with his/her doctors, treatment professionals, and sponsors to upgrade as need arises is a powerful tool for assisting in maintenance of recovery.

We have discussed warnings, signs, and triggers of relapse and ways to prevent or minimize its occurrence. In spite of these efforts, the reality is, relapse does happen. When it occurs, the proactive response is not to engage in self-blame or judgment. Life in treatment is about progress, not perfection. We learn from the experience, get back on treatment plan with all the help we can muster from our team of treatment professionals, and move on. Relapse could be a learning process that we could share with others to help them in their recovery.

6.10 Intervention Plan

Counselor and patient develop early relapse intervention. The deliberation entails what action to take if the patient begins to use alcohol and/or drugs. This insightful process serves as a motivation factor for the patient to stay sober and provide a safety net in case relapse occurs. The self-assessment that follows as a consequence of the process promotes increased level of conscious understanding and acceptance of situations and events that have led to past relapses. Also, it enhances coping skills, self-regulation, self-knowledge, and awareness in the management of relapse warnings and effectively arresting or reducing the risk of relapse.

Case Study: Recipe for Relapse (From Author's Clinical Diary)

Lonnie, a brilliant engineering student at Portland State University (PSU) attended Insight Inc. and other counseling and support programs. Family history reveals maternal grandfather, a recovering alcoholic; his mother, a chronic functional alcohol abuser; and a junior brother in recovery from heroin addiction. Without a doubt, Lonnie has a deep-seated genetic predisposition to drug addiction. He struggles with alcoholism and depression for which he is receiving treatment. His regular attendance to our counseling sessions and other programs has kept him sober for over 4 weeks after ending a rocky five-year relationship with a girl who also struggles with alcoholism. Both used alcohol heavily through the tumultuous relationship.

Lonnie met a girl on the Internet. He decided to move to Corvallis, Oregon, about 84 miles away from his base in Portland, Oregon. He intended to transfer to Oregon State University (OSU) in Corvallis. His reason was to get closer to the new relationship so he could get to know her better. He was aware that a new relationship in early recovery could trigger a relapse. We had this discussion in a group counseling session. However, it was a choice he made.

After 3 weeks in his new relationship, it ended abruptly. He blamed it on incompatibility. He claimed, "We were like day and night. She was not close to the script she communicated." His hope of securing a job was dashed because every job interview he attended was unsuccessful. The overwhelming stress, layers of unresolved emotional issues around relationships, intense depression, and financial hardship took a toll. He relapsed. He went binge drinking at a bar. He resided at a center in Corvallis that has a strict policy on alcohol and drug use. The smell of alcohol from his breath was picked up by a residence staff member who reported him to the authorities. His urine testing was positive for alcohol and he was kicked out of the building. He returned to Portland. At the time of this writing, he is actively working toward his recovery. He would need to seek tools that once kept him sober: a physician consultation to review treatment of his depression, a reassessment, and renewed treatment plan for his alcoholism; regular attendance and active participation in counseling and support group programs. Also, he will benefit from consultation with a relationship expert to resolve his issues around relationships.

The red flags or warning signs that eventually trigger the relapse are reflected in this case study. Such red flags are a new relationship in early recovery and after 4 weeks of the breakup of a prior turbulent relationship, and the grief related to loss of these relationships. Loss of income from pressure trying to relocate and find a job was contributory to the stressful situation. These stressors, combined with related anxiety and depression, constitute the triggers of relapse.

7 Crisis Intervention

Alcoholism and drug addiction is characterized by excessive intake depicted by "loss of control." A close analogy is the cancerous state of cells where cell replication is "out of control."

This behavior dynamic is not only unhealthy but often on a crisis-oriented collision course. The risk of fatality is high and intervention is crucial. This chapter focuses on crisis intervention in general because clinical symptoms and presentation of drug addiction are sometimes life threatening and multifaceted.

Crisis is an acute emotional reaction to a powerful stimulus or critical event: a stress-induced event with gradual to abrupt onset. Often, it is not the event, but the client's subjective perception of the event as acute and overwhelming. The immediate response to the situation is the absolute evasion or minimization of the consequence of the crisis.

Conditions that precipitate a crisis could be a result of stressful, hazardous situations, or perceptions of the situation as disruptive and emotionally upsetting. Each patient has variable ability to manage a crisis according to the constraints of limited coping mechanisms. This subjective assessment of a situation appears to be a highly intense and fear-oriented contemplation of impending calamity which culminates in chaotic reactions.

These cascades of emotional and psychological destabilization often presage intense cravings for alcohol or drug abuse. The complication that ensues usually compromises rational thinking and releases uncontrollable emotions. Factors that aggravate crisis reaction include exposure that generates more powerful reactions. Longer periods of intense incidents may exacerbate reactions. But increased support from family and friends and additional helpful resources can mitigate the intensity of the reaction.

Crisis Intervention: A relatively short but active period of interrupting an individual or group's life situation to eliminate or minimize the critical stress and restore normalcy or de-escalate the emotional turmoil.

We must be cognizant of the fact that crisis intervention is not necessarily a type of psychotherapy or a substitute. It is a process of multidisciplinary frameworks that, when appropriately and effectively applied, intercept an acute emergency state of life situation to restore a stabilized condition.

7.1 Crisis Intervention Primary Principles

Proximity: Familiar environment is reassuring for the victim.

Immediacy: In an acute/emergency situation, urgency is the watch word that demands immediate action for effective intervention.

Practical Skills and Clinical Management of Alcoholism and Drug Addiction.
DOI: http://dx.doi.org/10.1016/B978-0-12-398518-7.00007-9

Expectancy: A crisis intervention provider should be familiar, optimistic, and hopeful for the client, even when a situation seems hopeless. The therapist should instill a sense of hope and provide encouraging words for victims.

Brevity: This is of the essence. A swift moment of intervention might be a saving grace.

Simplicity: "Keep it simple." Complex processes might not serve well in a critical time for successful victim management. Providers often have regular practices in preparation for crisis intervention. At some point, intervention becomes a "reflex action." I can confirm this high degree of readiness in my clinical experience in the emergency room.

Creativity: The art of innovation and improvisation can be an essential part of readiness and simplicity in crisis intervention.

Practical: Every action must be practical. Otherwise, it has no place in a critical situation where life is at stake and time is of the essence.

7.2 Crisis Intervention Goals

To control the crisis event, stabilize the victim, and consequently reduce or eliminate reaction to crisis.

To counteract the impact of the event on those involved, and put to rest the chaos and extreme distress to the barest minimum.

To organize and deploy resources necessary to effectively resolve stressful situations and the victim's trauma. The resuscitation process will primarily attempt to de-escalate the situation within a limited time. This can preserve life and possibly move further toward achieving a stable condition and developing appropriate referrals for management continuum.

Crisis intervention services are provided in early episodes of crisis within the first 4–6 weeks. However, these could be extended, especially when the causes and reactions are still unresolved within the critical noxious stimulus and reactive severity. That these services are essential cannot be over-emphasized. As humans, we are vulnerable at any time in our lives. How individuals react to crises can be uncomfortable and distressing. The suddenness of crisis and individual failures to cope are the common scenario. Crises are temporary and often subside in 24–72 h. They could, however, be lethal if intervention is late or improperly applied. Adequate support often mitigates distress and a critical situation. Here is a list of common services essential for crisis management.

7.3 Crisis Intervention Services

Emergency psychiatric assessments,
General crisis assessments,
Immediate supportive intervention: food, water, and shelter,

Crisis telephone hotlines,
Walk-in crisis clinics,
Family support services,
Referrals for depression, suicidal ideation, drug abuse, violence, AIDS, child abuse, sexual assault, psychiatric emergencies, significant-other battering, and crime victimization,
Poison control centers,
Mobile crisis clinic,
Individual crisis support,
Peer support (paraprofessional) programs,
Group crisis support for both large and small groups,
Immediate crisis counseling.

The lives of alcoholics or drug addicts are often plagued by crises. Crisis intervention providers are equipped with tools to manage the varieties of causes of these emergencies. This ranges from emotional and psychological breakdown to physical and/or physiological crises: aspiration, pneumonitis, asphyxia, or acute cardiac malfunction to comatose state due to oral or intravenous abuse of psychoactive drugs. Crisis management entails preparedness that is broad based and time prudent primarily because it is crucial to the revival of victims.

Strategic approach should be put into consideration: the victim and nature of pathologies; the type of intervention that is adequate; and proper timing, a relative factor determined by victim's acceptance of help and situation that requests assistance from witnesses and/or family members to expedite the vital management. This assistance may reflect issues that may be related to prior incidence that results in the present crisis.

These identified factors make it simple and easy to dispatch the right and specific resources in crisis intervention management.

All should be advised to dial 911 in case of emergency and explain the situation. The appropriate crisis intervention provider will be sent.

A *real crisis* that remains is that addiction is seen by too many as a reprehensible moral weakness, instead of being recognized as a disease or a medical condition. Despite recent advances in treatment methods, social stigma and misconceptions about addiction still persist. As more humane laws are enacted to support the medical consensus, public perceptions about addiction will change. Family, friends, employers, health care professionals, and behavioral therapists must become proactive in educating the public. At present, many who suffer from real and pervasive consequences of addiction tend to lead secret lives, obsessed with fears that their "weakness" may be revealed. Until such time as we can dispel these stereotypes and dispense with prejudice and discrimination, addicts and their families will suffer needlessly. And we, as a people, will be diminished by their pain and reaction. The stigmatization of these victims must end. We owe it to our families, neighbors, neighborhoods ... and to ourselves.

Inspired by: *Life Events, Clinical Experience, and Intellectual Curiosity*

Samuel B. Obembe, M.B;B.S., C.A.D.C.

Serenity Creed

I'm aware of predispositions to my medical condition:

- Genetic variance
- Heredity
- Genetic mutation
- Vulnerability due to *mental disorders
  *negative environmental factors
  *parental abuse and/or neglect
  *other causes.
  But I must accept Responsibility for
  *use, abuse, addiction, and consequence.

And with *commitment to treatment and a healthy lifestyle

*regular attendance at support group meetings
*in regular contact or company of sponsors, positive individuals, peer groups, and family members

I will achieve Self-Discovery, Willpower, and Self-Determination that pave the way to my Sobriety and Recovery.
IN ANY SITUATION, HAPPY OR SAD, STRESSFUL OR PEACEFUL, DRINKING OR USING IS NOT AN OPTION.

Bibliography

Atkinson, R. (2001). In A. M. Gurnack & N. Osgood (Eds.), *Treating Alcohol and Drug Use in the Elderly*. NY: Springer Publishing.

Burns, D. D. (1999). *Feeling good: The new mood therapy*. New York, NY: Penguin Books.

Chambers, R. A., Sajdyk, T. J., Conroy, S. K., Lafuze, J. E., Fitz, S. D. & Shekhar, A. (2007). Neonatal amygdala lesions: Co-occuring impact in Social fear-related behaviour and Cocaine Sensitization in adult rats.

Coombs, R. H. (2005). *Addiction counseling review: Preparing for comprehensive, certification and licensing examinations*. Hillsdale, NJ: Lawrence Erlbaum Associates.

Edwards, G., & Gross, M. M. (1976). Alcohol dependence: Provisional description of a clinical syndrome. *The British Medical Journal, 1*, 1058–1061.

Erickson, C. K. (2007). *The science of addiction*. New York, NY: W.W. Norton & Company.

Graham, K., Saunders, S. J., Flower, M., Timney, C., White-Campbell, M., & Pietropaolo, A. (1995). *Addiction treatment for older adults*. New York, NY: Routledge.

Heath, A. C., Jardine, R., & Martin, N. G. (1989). Interactive effects of genotype and social environment on alcohol consumption in female twins. *Journal of Studies on Alcohol, 50*(1), 38–48.

Keri, J. *Behavioral neuroscience*. OHSU Research Scientist, VA Medical Centre.

Kosanke, N., Maqura, S., Staines, G., Foote, J., & DeLuca, A. (2002). Feasibility of matching alchol patients to ASAM levels of care. *The American Journal on Addiction, 11*, 124–134.

King, A. C., Volpicelli, J. R., Frazer, A., & O'Brien, C. P. (1997). Effect of Naltrexone on subjective alcohol response in subjects at high and low risk for future alcohol dependence. *Psychopharmacology, 129*, 613–615.

Linehan, M. M. (1993). *Cognitive behavioral treatment of borderline personality disorder*. New York, NY: The Guilford Press.

McLellan, A. T., Cacciola, J. S., & Alterman, A. I. (2004). The ASI as a still developing instrument. *Response to Mäkelä. Addiction, 99*, 411–412.

Miller, W. R., & Rollnick, S. (Eds.). (1991). *Motivational Interviewing: preparing people to change addictive behaviour*. New York: Guilford Press.

Miller, W. R., & Carroll, K. M. (2006). *Rethinking substance abuse: What the science shows and what we should do about it*. New York, NY: The Guilford Press.

Morse, R.M., & Flavin, D. K. (1992). Definition of addiction. *Journal of the American Medical Association (JAMA), 68*(8).

Nature. *Neuroscience, 7*, 699–700. doi:10.1038/nn1271

Oregon Department of Corrections (2008). Research and Evaluation Unit-Scorecard-ad_comp_by_program_2008.rtf.

Ravalec, V., Mallendi, & Paicheler, A. (2007). *Iboga: The visionary root of African shamanism*. Rochester, VT: Park Street Press, Inner Traditions/Bear and Company.

Substance Abuse and Mental Health Services Administration (SAMHSA). 2002–2010 National Survey on Drug use and Health-an annual Survey of approximately 67,500 people throughout the country who are over the age of 12.

Shaw, S. C. (2004). *Alcohol and Drug Abuse Prevention & Treatment Program. Drinking & driving with alcohol level calculator—Better life*. Alexandria, VA: NAADAC.

Storie, M. (2005). *Basics of addiction counseling: Desk reference and study guide*. Alexandria, VA: NAADAC.

Turner, W. M., Turner, K. H, Reif, S., Gutowski, W. E., & Gastfriend, D. R. (1999). Drug and Alcohol dependence. *Feasibility of multidimensional substance abuse treatment matching: automating the ASAM patient placement*, 35–43.

Werblin, J. M. (2011). Genetic research and addiction. Retrieved January 26, 2010, from Treatment Centers. <www.treatment-centers.net/addiction-genetics.html/>.

Wolstein, J., Gastpar, M., Finkbeiner, T., Heinrich, C., Heitkamp, R., & Poehlke, T., et al. (2009). A randomized, open-label trial comparing methadone and levo-alpha-acetylmethadol (LAAM) in maintenance treatment of opioid addiction. *Pharmacopsychiatry, 42*(1), 1–8.

WHO (1992–94). *ICD-10 International statistical classification of diseases and related health problems*, Tenth Revision Volumes 1–3. Geneva: World Health Organization.